THE
BAREFOOT
HORSE

THE
BAREFOOT
HORSE

An Introduction to Barefoot
Hoof Care and Hoof Boots

LUCY NICHOLAS

J. A. ALLEN · LONDON

*Dedicated to the memory of my dear mother Val, who introduced
me to horses at a very early age.*

First published in Great Britain in 2012
J. A. Allen
Clerkenwell House
Clerkenwell Green
London ECIR OHT
J. A. Allen is an imprint of Robert Hale Limited
www.allenbooks.co.uk.

ISBN 978 0 85131 987 2

British Library Cataloguing in Publication Data
A catalogue record for this book is available from the British Library

Design and typesetting by Paul Saunders
Edited by Martin Diggle

Photographs by, or property of the author, except for the following: pp.13 (top left), 35, 41 (top and bottom left), 42, 46, 57 (top and right), 58 and 59 (lower) by Dawn Saunders, pp.26, 43 (right), 48, 49 and 85 by Ros Jones, pp.93 and 94 by Tina Steiner, p. 19 by Sarah Addyman, p.24 by Easycare Inc/Duncan McLaughlin, p.64 by Easycare Inc, p.92 by AGC Photography, p.16 by Karen Corr, p.38 (right) by DLT Photography, p.89 by Mandi Edwards, p.62 by Lisa Hill, p.12 by Jaime Jackson/AANHCP, p.88 by Steven Leigh and p.41 (bottom right) byLiz Lilliman.

Line illustrations by Carole Vincer

Printed by Craft Print International Ltd, Singapore

Disclaimer of Liability

CONTENTS

ACKNOWLEDGEMENTS

I would like to thank the following people for their help with providing information and images for this book:

Sarah Addyman
Amanda and Mac
Kathy Carter
Mike Chawke RF(BngC), MF(IMFA), CE-F
Vicky Clink
Angela Corner – Rockcruncher's Barefoot Trimming Services
Karen Corr
Debbie Crosoer
Rohan Fox – Hoofworks
Ros Jones MRCVS
Steven Leigh – Nature's Way Hoof Care
Liz Lilliman
Jamie Jackson and Jill Willis AANHCP
Jessica Orr – Natural Barefoot Trimming
Dr Mischa Rose
Dawn Saunders – Barefoot Works
Tina Steiner
Yvonne Welz

Thanks, also, to my husband David, for taking some of the photos and for his overall support, and to everyone who contributed to the studies I undertook during research.

Chapter ONE

HOOF PROTECTION THROUGH THE AGES

ISTORY IS AMBIGUOUS WITH regard to the domestication of horses, and although horses appeared in Palaeolithic cave art as early as *circa* 30,000 BC, these were wild horses and were likely to have been hunted as food.

The most likely date of domestication and use of the horse as a means of transport is somewhere between 5000–3500 BC (during the Bronze Age). The most compelling evidence comes from archaeological discoveries in the Steppes.[1] For much of this period, no thought was ever given to protecting horses' hooves. Xenophon's book *The Art of Horsemanship*[2] is one of the earliest recorded manuscripts that refers to the care of horses' hooves, and the famous Greek military commander and historian even discusses conditioning horses' feet by using river stone in their stables, and also talks about equine diet.

This indicates that, even 2300 years ago, horses were being subjected to unnatural living conditions. However, there is no evidence currently to suggest that Greeks shod their horses, so we are left to presume they must have developed a system of conditioning their horses' feet, or protecting them well enough without metal shoes. There is, however, substantive evidence that horses suffered from hoof pathologies long before shoes were invented. For example, there is evidence that laminitis has been noted historically since the Roman era.[3]

Early challenges faced by the horse

Two of the most important challenges that horses faced were confinement and often a change from their natural diet. For convenience, working horses were more likely to be kept in stables or other small areas close to human habitation and their diet was far from ideal; they were no longer permitted to browse to find the natural plants and herbs they needed for optimum health. This move towards confining horses for long periods, often standing in their own urine and dung, coupled with a poor diet, gave rise to much poorer horn quality that was less able to withstand the hours of work these horses were often required to do.

Horses living in the wild, such as these Dartmoor ponies, have adapted to the soft, wet yet sometimes rocky terrain.

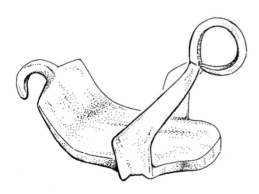

The Roman hipposandal.

In Britain, horses were initially used to working mainly on soft or forgiving surfaces, but the Roman invasion and the subsequent building of the first roads led to horses becoming sore or lame when asked to pull or carry heavy loads on these unforgiving, yet practical surfaces. By this time, some thought had been given to equine footwear, and the Romans had developed the hipposandal. However, while this had originally been thought of as a rudimentary horseshoe, a reconstruction by the UK's Channel 4 TV programme *Time Team* found it to be very crude and difficult to move in, leading to the assumption it was more likely to have been an early emergency boot for pathological use, rather than standard footwear for covering any distance.

The birth of farriery

Although it is widely documented that the practice of nailing metal to a horse's hoof for protection began around 400–500 AD, it was not widely practised until 1100–1200 AD, because of the high value of iron. According to historian Dr Mischa Rose, shoeing was most likely to have been introduced at the time of the Crusades and the development of the cavalry in Western Europe. Dr Rose explains:

> People develop or adopt a technology to solve a problem, usually. If you have a pack horse or a farm horse and it isn't 100% sound, you can rest it or beat it until it plods on, but you can't do that with a highly trained horse that you're intending to sit on as a fighting platform. It needs to be able to move, and to turn, and not to stumble if it hits a stone, because your life depends on it.[4]

She continues to explain that the terrain these Crusaders' horses would have been expected to cover would have been vastly different from the soft European pastures. In addition, with a population of highly skilled metalworkers and armourers serving the Crusades, the (already pre-existing) technology for shoeing suddenly became both available and necessary to keep these highly valuable animals sound enough to go into battle.

In 1356, the Lord Mayor of London, Henry Pykard, summoned before him all the farriers of the capital city to deal with the many offences and damages that had been committed by 'people not wise therein'. These were lay-people who kept forges in the city and meddled with practices that they did not understand, to the greater detriment of the horse. From this event, the Worshipful Company of Farriers was born. However, it was not until 1975 that actual legislation was applied to this area in the form of the Farriers' (Registration) Act 1975 (later amended in 1977) whereby Parliament affirmed that the Company should have 'the general functions of securing adequate standards of competence and conduct' among farriers and the duty of 'promoting, encouraging and advancing the art and science of farriery' and education in connection with farriery.[5]

Is a crescent-shaped piece of steel really the answer?

During the more recent historical period, which led to advancements such as the regulation of farriers working on our horses' hooves, society has made numerous changes in many areas. Commercial air travel and modern medical developments are just two examples of conveniences that were mere speculation just a century or so ago, and mankind continues to take huge steps forward in finding new materials and improvements in every walk of life. Yet, the practice of nailing a crescent-shaped piece of steel onto a horse's hoof has remained largely unchanged since the practice began around a thousand years ago.

Some may argue this is because it is the best method of protecting a horse's hoof from wear, but if you were to be presented with solving an issue of protecting a flexible, shock-absorbing structure from the abrasive nature of a road in our modern age, would a hard, rigid, concussive material like metal really be the first solution to spring to mind? Development in materials in the last fifty or so years now allows us to create flexible, durable materials such as those used in car tyres and high-performance athletic shoes. Some of these materials have found their way into the construction of horseshoes, although not in mainstream farriery; often because of the cost of manufacturing small quantities.

Plastics and rubber have been used to try to reduce weight, improve traction and reduce the concussion traditionally associated with metal shoes, but they are still permanently attached to the horse's foot through the means of glue or nails (the source of restriction); the sole remains suspended in most cases and the preparation of the hoof for the shoe largely remains the same.

Should horses be kept as near as possible to their wild state?

In our lives, it is widely accepted that modern human habits, such as eating excessive amounts of 'junk food' and exercising less, are significantly detrimental to our health and potentially our lifespan. We are being told by experts that we should do our best to return to an increasingly fruit- and vegetable-rich, low fat, lower sugar diet, coupled with regular exercise to keep our bodies in good order and help prevent disease. The same thing has been happening in the horse world, and with the aid of modern research, many studies demonstrate the need for horses to be kept as near as possible to the wild state in which their bodies evolved to thrive.

Obviously, our domesticated horses are not wild and their lifestyle is far removed from their wild ancestors, but much information can be gained from studying feral horse populations to see how the horse lives naturally, and adapting the findings to fit in with our modern existence. It has long being said by knowledgeable farriers that nailing a shoe to a hoof is convenient for the owner, but has detrimental effects on their horse.

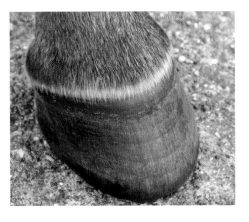

A picture of health: domestic horses thrive on a regime that is as close as practical to the wild state that their body has evolved to live in. Beautiful hooves are just one health benefit to be seen when you keep your horse in a more natural way.

Experts tend to agree that horses should not be shod unless there is a need for it, and this need is usually the owners' need, not the horse's! It is also suggested by a great many farriers that there should be periods to rest the hooves from the effects of shoeing – a practice often demonstrated by hunt or event horses that are worked hard for the winter, but roughed off in the summer months without shoes.

The shod verses unshod debate has stimulated a large amount of research that is being carried out by vets, farriers and other knowledgeable individuals, and this is leading us to believe that many of the ailments that we so often see in our horses should not be seen as an inevitable result of

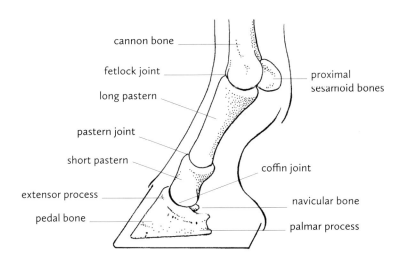

cannon bone

fetlock joint

long pastern

pastern joint

short pastern

extensor process

pedal bone

proximal sesamoid bones

coffin joint

navicular bone

palmar process

The structure of the lower leg.

the work we do with them. As our horses age, we have grown to accept the possibility of problems arising such as arthritis, back trouble, navicular syndrome, ringbone and stiffness, to name but a few; yet so many of these problems are rarely if ever seen within the aged horses in feral herds.

The owner's duty of care

Shoeing has now been a part of the horse world for so long that often horse owners are not aware of the hoof their horses were born to grow. Metal shoes affect the way the hoof grows and develops, and it is important for horse owners to recognise what a healthy, balanced hoof looks like, be it shod or barefoot. Many horse owners feel the hoof is the responsibility of their farrier but, ultimately, the owner has a duty of care to their horse to understand enough to be able to make the right choices about their horse's hoof care.

The easiest way to see a healthy, natural hoof that has not had any human intervention is to look at the hooves of the feral horse population. One of the most famous images, that almost every person interested in barefoot hoof care will have seen, is that of a wild mustang cadaver first published by Jamie Jackson, founder of the Association for the Advancement of Natural Horse Care Practices (AANHCP).

The iconic wild mustang hoof, © Jaime Jackson, courtesy of the AANHCP. Jamie is one of the pioneers of the barefoot movement and his famous wild mustang hoof image shows the form upon which the 'wild horse' trim methods are based.

This hoof is the epitome of strength and speed in a wild horse. Hard, smooth walls bevelled for the quickest of breakover with a deeply concave sole and a wide, fleshy frog make this hoof more effective at carrying this horse effortlessly for miles on end with the least amount of effort, or risk of injury. By contrast, even a very correctly shod hoof shows a number of differences, including a much longer hoof capsule, less concavity, longer heels and, of course, the most obvious and unavoidable difference; the way the hoof is loading. A bare hoof distributes the weight of the horse on most terrain across the entire sole and inner wall, whereas in the shod hoof, the only option on most surfaces is to load peripherally on the outer wall, with the frog and sole usually only able to contact the ground on much softer surfaces.

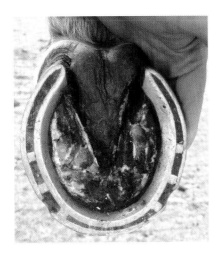

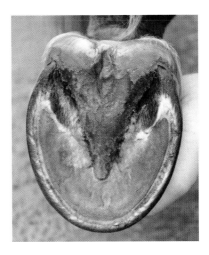

FAR LEFT *A well-shod hoof, but it is clear to see how the shoe is preventing the natural weight distribution across the sole on all but the softest of surfaces that the hoof thrives on.*

LEFT *Characteristics of a healthy hoof include an open heel, large frog and heel bulbs and a naturally short toe and heel, with a tight white line.*

'No foot, no horse'

Almost every horse owner will have heard the old adage 'no foot, no horse' at some point in their lives, and this demonstrates the universal agreement of how important strong, healthy hooves are to the survival of our horses. Horses' hooves are constantly growing and changing, forever adapting to the changes in the horse's environment. The hoof reacts to every step the horse takes; the terrain dictates the amount of wear and shock the hoof endures, which stimulates the hoof to adapt. Most domestic horses' hooves do not have the stimulus afforded by covering between 20 and 30 miles of varied terrain a day and this lack of stimulus, coupled with a diet that is often too rich in sugars, results in a hoof capsule that is prone to becoming weak and overgrown.

Traditionally, domestic horses living without shoes would normally be trimmed every 8–12 weeks which, without the necessary stimulation and wear, allows the hooves to grow much longer than they would naturally. In these circumstances the horse's systems will try to counteract the unwanted horn that is lifting the hoof off the ground by slowing down and altering the angle of growth. Quarter cracks may appear and chunks of hoof may even break away as the hooves try to rebalance themselves and allow the soles to become more active. In order to counteract this detrimental effect to the hoof, most modern barefoot horses are trimmed every 2–4 weeks. Owners who feel sufficiently confident to maintain their horses' hooves in between professional trims may even increase this frequency to once a week, especially during times of extreme growth, such as spring and autumn.

By trimming tiny amounts on such a regular basis, we are able to simulate fairly accurately the wear the horse's hoof would naturally receive, and the balance and growth of the hoof will remain pretty consistent. Arguably, one of the best ways to help your horse maintain well-trimmed, balanced hooves is to allow him to 'self-trim' by providing abrasive terrain when riding, and at pasture. Most horses will wear the hoof they need for their individual conformation when this occurs, although it is always important to keep a close eye on the balance to ensure that it is correct and no imbalances are creeping in. For example, riding a horse on the road will ensure that the hooves remain worn, but roads often have a camber, which may cause a horse to wear an imbalance that needs to be rectified manually at regular intervals.

When a horse is shod, it is obviously impossible to trim on such a regular basis; the lack of such regular trimming is one reason why it is common to see problems such as flares (which are characterised by a deviation outwards at the bottom of the hoof), especially at the quarters, under-run heels, and also a much slower growth rate. Typically, a shod horse will have grown down an entire hoof capsule in around 12 months, while a correctly maintained barefoot horse will usually have completed a growth cycle in 6–8 months (depending on the amount of stimulation). Regular trimming also ensures that the horse is never subjected to severe angle changes within the hoof capsule, which can potentially cause strains to structures further up the leg.

Hoof balance and structure

It is important that every horse owner should learn to recognise the basics of a balanced hoof, whether shod or barefoot. Balance is not only essential to the health and function of the hoof capsule; the balance of the hoof can affect the tendons and joints of the limbs and even the horse's back, so we owe it to our horses to understand enough to ensure we employ the right professional to care for their feet.

Balance will vary between horses, and even between individual hooves, particularly if a horse has a conformational issue, such as cow hocks or pigeon toes. There are certain ideals that characterise a 'barefoot trim', but do take time to talk to your trimmer or farrier to understand more about your individual horse's needs.

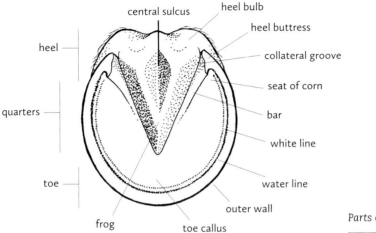

Parts of the hoof.

Features of a barefoot hoof

The horse's hoof is an amazing structure, and grows continuously like our own nails; hence the need for regular trimming. A healthy barefoot hoof is characterised by a naturally short heel and toe, and the sole of a healthy hoof is usually concave. The frog should look large, and extend roughly two-thirds of the way from the heel to the toe. There is often a noticeable rim of sole just inside the white line (particularly at the toe), which is located under the outer edge of the pedal bone and forms one of the significant weight-bearing structures along with the frog, heel and wall. Another significant feature of a barefoot hoof is the bevelled edge (sometimes referred to as the mustang roll) which is applied to the outer rim of the hoof wall, to help prevent chipping and reduce the likelihood of splitting.

Some trimming methods advocate a heavy roll to emulate the appearance of the wild hoof described earlier, while others use a more conservative version, but all acknowledge the importance of this feature within a working, bare hoof. Most people, when thinking of a horse's hoof, presume that the outer wall is required to be long enough to lift the sole off the ground (known as peripheral loading) on most surfaces in order to protect the sole. This is almost certainly because most people are used to seeing horses in shoes that naturally create an artificially longer 'outer wall'. Studies have, however, shown that the sole is an important part of the weight-bearing process. Stimulating the sole causes the horn to thicken and become more concave, and the internal structures will sit higher in the hoof capsule as a result (and are thus better protected).

When a horse is travelling across soft, pebbly or dusty terrain, the barefoot hoof will load across the solar plane and inner wall fairly evenly. On terrain such as roads, the hoof will load primarily on the hoof wall and frog. On level ground, the horse will usually land heel first; as the foot rolls through the step, the elastic frog will give with the horse's weight to allow the hoof capsule to expand, helping to dissipate shock. The internal structures are pressed downwards into the corium (the vascular bundle between the sole and the bony structures above, and out of which the frog and sole grow), which squeezes the blood through the veins. This sponge-like structure will then expand to draw blood back into it, as the horse takes the weight back off the hoof.

Flare is a common occurrence in pasture-kept horses, but is usually detrimental to the function of the hoof capsule and should be addressed by your hoof care professional appropriately, especially in the working barefoot horse.

The hoof wall is made up of keratin, a fibrous protein which is also a constituent of substances such as human hair. The outer wall is made up of many densely packed tubules, which makes it extremely strong. The inner wall is made up from the same tubules, but they're less dense; the majority of the inner wall is made up of inter-tubular horn that allows the inner wall to act as an elastic layer between the rigid outer wall and the internal structures. This is why it is important to trim regularly, to ensure that the hoof is able to grow strong, straight walls with no unnatural 'flare'.

Flare is characterised by a deviation outwards at the bottom of the hoof and can occur for a number of reasons, including excessive growth for the amount of wear or trimming it receives, the horse's conformation, movement or another stress factor. Every horse will have his own ideal hoof angle (when viewed from the side), as breeds and horses within those breeds differ so much. Therefore, the traditional guideline of a 45 to 50 degree angle for the forefeet, and a 50 to 55 degree angle for the hind feet, is now viewed less strictly, as increasing numbers of experts agree that each horse's optimal hoof angle differs. Hoof/pastern angle is one way of assessing the correct angle for an individual, whereby the pastern bone remains in line with the dorsal angle of the hoof when the horse is standing square.

One useful method of assessing correct hoof angle is to look at the inch of new hoof growth below the coronet band and see if the angle of this new growth matches the angle of the older growth below. Deviations either way are often a sign of imbalance within the hoof capsule, and your trimmer will usually work towards achieving a consistent angle within the hoof.

References

1. www.gsa.confex.com/gsa/2006AM/finalprogram/abstract_116407.htm

2. Xenophon, *circa* 430–354 BC.

3. www.ncbi.nlm.nih.gov/pubmed/10568001

4. Quote provided by historian Dr Mischa Rose, as told to author.

5. www.wcf.org.uk/the_company

Chapter TWO

WHAT IS BAREFOOT?

BAREFOOT IN THE MODERN SENSE is generally regarded as a term used to describe a horse or pony that is able to perform anything that the owner would like to do, without the need for permanent hoof protection. One name synonymous with modern barefoot is Dr Hiltrud Strasser; her name is very well-known for many reasons, but unfortunately not all positive.

Horses evolved a means of swift, reliable passage across all terrain in the form of hooves, and domestic horses are no different if their body is kept in a natural way to allow this mechanism to work to its full potential.

Dr Strasser is a German veterinarian who, for over 20 years, has been studying and researching lameness and other common health problems of domestic horses. In 1993, she opened the Institute for Hoof Health and the European School for Hoof Orthopedics (ESHOP) in Tuebingen, Germany. Her trimming procedure was one of the earliest but most highly controversial trims, using very aggressive techniques which led to some highly publicised cases, including in the UK, where the Strasser trim was replicated unsuccessfully. This resulted in a large amount of bad publicity, which did cast doubt for a period over the idea of keeping horses barefoot at all. However, I feel it is important to recognise her work and her ideas about natural horse-keeping (out of stalls), as they are still relevant to our barefoot horses today.

Journalist Yvonne Welz explained in an article that she wrote for the popular and unbiased online barefoot resource, www.thehorseshoof.com:

> Everyone who teaches about, trims, owns, or enjoys naturally-trimmed barefoot horses today owes a huge debt of gratitude to Dr Strasser, as she is a major player in the origin of our modern barefoot. Our modern barefoot world was actually created when Jaime Jackson brought Dr Strasser to the United States for the first time.... Many names you will be probably more familiar with, such as Jamie Jackson, Pete Ramey and K.C. La Pierre to name but a very few, took this idea of barefoot horses very much to heart and as a result, produced their own, very different ideas based eventually on other far less invasive methods, much more suited to maintaining hooves in the 'real world'.[6]

Can all horses go barefoot?

This is a hotly-contested subject amongst hoof care professionals, and one answer frequently heard is that: 'Every horse can go barefoot, but not every owner can!' The reasons for this argument are that shoes are a convenience for the owner that allow the hooves to be maintained in such a way that little needs to be done by the owner to keep the horse sound enough to work in the immediate future on most surfaces.

Barefoot management, however, requires that hooves are kept in prime condition, and some horses will be harder to maintain in a barefoot regime than others, depending on their background. The transition of horses with less than ideal hooves to a barefoot regime may be a job that requires time, patience and a little investment, at least in the beginning and, in all cases, the management of a barefoot horse may not suit the owner's requirements for practices that are predominantly chosen for convenience (such as stabling).

Banjo, a 6-year-old traditional cob has never been shod but is able to enjoy doing everything in life that a shod horse does.

Some professionals cite that some horses are unable to go barefoot owing to genetics, structural or conformational problems, and that it is fairer to such horses to remain shod. However, the vast majority of hoof care professionals will say that there are very few horses that do not have the potential to lead sound working lives without metal shoes on, but that some will be harder and take longer than others to change over, and there may be some that will always need another form of hoof protection when working (i.e. hoof boots) in order for them to remain comfortable.

Every horse is an individual, and it is not just hoof quality that needs to be considered (as often horses that go bare improve beyond recognition within a relatively short period). Factors that affect the success of a new barefoot regime have to be considered carefully. Horses with very poor hooves will need to be kept in conditions as close to ideal as possible to succeed, whereas horses that have good hooves to begin with may need very little changing in order to adapt quickly to a life without shoes.

Considering the options

When considering whether your horse could become barefoot, it is best to get the opinion of at least one professional – or more, if you are uncertain or unhappy about the views of the first. There is no harm in asking hoof care professionals from different affiliations either, as every horse is an individual and both horse and owner need to be comfortable with whatever path is chosen to maintain the horse's hooves.

The decision may be easy for some owners, as their horse may already have strong enough feet to require little adaptation to become able to cope with the required work when barefoot. This is more likely to be the case if the horse is being sympathetically shod, and is being kept in a natural environment promoting movement, along with being fed a good gut- and hoof-friendly diet. A horse being kept more artificially with, for example, a high-sugar diet and restricted turnout, may have much poorer quality horn to start with. There would need to be a significant change in the latter's management system and the use of hoof boots in order to produce the healthiest hoof that the horse is capable of growing.

Looking after a barefoot horse is no harder than a shod horse for most owners once they have established a new routine, but owners should consider their situation before deciding whether barefoot is the best option for their horse. The three major points that will be cited by the vast majority of barefoot advocates when referring to a successful barefoot horse are:

1. A good, regular trimming schedule.

2. A good diet based on food the horse's body evolved to thrive on.

3. Exercise, including encouraging natural movement in the field and little or no confinement.

Many barefoot horses are kept in less than optimum conditions, yet still display the soundness and vigour of horses that are kept closer to the 'ideal'. This is usually because, although a compromise has been made (for example, stabling for a period during the day or night), this is counteracted by other factors (which, for example, could be that the horse is in training and covering many miles under saddle every day, making up for the lack of hoof stimulation when stabled).

One thing I say to people when they cannot decide whether they should take their horse barefoot, is to remember that the option of shoeing will always be there! However, the vast majority of people who go down the barefoot route with their horses say that they would never shoe again and wish they had done it years ago. Many first research the idea of barefoot as they have a horse that conventional or remedial shoeing has been unable to keep sound, but in seeing the difference it makes to that horse, they immediately remove the shoes of the sound horses they own as they want them to experience the benefits they can see come with living a life without metal shoes.

It is only recently that significant scientific research has been done into the effects of shoeing horses, but for a considerable time it has been acknowledged that it is a practice causing a degree of harm. One of the more famous quotes is from the very well-regarded text, *Hickman's Farriery*: 'Although shoes are necessary for continuous work on roads to prevent the hoof from being worn away by friction, they are detrimental because they interfere with the normal function of the foot.'

With the advent of modern hoof boots to prevent wear, the need to shoe is even further in question. There are, of course, those who question the scientific research, but the majority of farriers with the horse's best interests at heart agree that a horse's hoof is better left unshod whenever possible. So what 'pros and cons' are there for a barefoot horse that is properly trimmed and maintained, when compared to a well-shod horse?

Physical Factors

Concussion

The most obvious benefit to a hoof without shoes is probably the dramatic reduction in concussion that the hoof receives. When thinking of your own footwear, you would not expect to see a running shoe with a solid metal sole, or to drive a car with metal wheels; it would be ridiculous! The hoof capsule is designed to be a flexible unit, and the whole hoof is designed to dissipate the shock when the horse's foot hits the ground. With a shoe that prevents a lot of the natural movement and lifts it away from the ground, the hoof is at a big disadvantage. A 1983 University of Zurich dissertation by Swiss Scientist Luca Bein, based on his own studies, has been widely cited as finding that a hoof shod with a normal metal shoe lacks 60–80 per cent of its natural shock absorption properties. Bein is also said to have stated in the dissertation that: 'A shod foot moving on asphalt at a walk receives three times the impact force as an unshod foot moving on asphalt at a trot.' That's a lot of extra shock travelling not only through the hoof capsule, but up through the horse's leg and beyond, which could increase the horse's chance of developing arthritis, splints, side bone and many other stress-related conditions of the foot or limb.

Contraction

Contraction of the heel is usually a symptom of lack of stimulation of the back of the foot – arguably one of the most important areas of the hoof from a soundness point of view. In most healthy hooves, the horse will land fractionally heel first, giving the much-needed stimulation to the digital cushion in the back of the hoof (and also dissipating more shock). When in metal shoes (even if the horse is landing heel first) on most surfaces, the back of the heel and frog are not able to make proper contact with the ground, leading to a reduction in stimulation. This, in conjunction with reduced circulation, leads to a less-developed digital cushion. This is another widely acknowledged fact in the shoeing world, and thus shoes are applied to try to limit the contraction as much as possible. In fact the book *Modern Blacksmithing*, written as long ago as 1908, states: 'In most cases contraction is the result of shoeing and artificial living. Before the colt is shod, his hoofs are large and open-heeled, the quarters are spread out wide, and the foot on the under side is shaped like a saucer.'

LEFT *Look at the hoof-prints left by shod and barefoot horses and note in particular the absence of the depth (if any) of frog print in the shod hoof. The frog not only acts as a hinge within the hoof mechanism, but also allows the horse to gain feedback about the ground he is walking on, and gives excellent grip.*

ABOVE *Hoof care is important from an early age. Regular trimming from just a few weeks after the foal is born will ensure he will grow up with the best possible feet and limbs, as subtle imbalances are not allowed to creep in.*

Balance

The bare hoof is given the opportunity to wear correctly, given correct management. Small, regular trims ensure that no major angle changes take place and replicate natural wear. A shod horse is totally dependent on the farrier trimming and shoeing with exact balance, as there is no chance for wear of the hoof capsule once the shoe has been applied. Farriers are only human and, often with so many horses to shoe in a day, a good farrier is the first to admit that physically it is difficult to balance and shoe every single horse 100 per cent accurately, especially those nearer the end of the day or those that fidget.

Circulation

When I was younger, I remember being taught that my ponies' hooves should feel cold, and that heat was a sign of a problem. Years later, when I touch my barefoot horses' warm hooves, it makes far more sense to me now that a structure rich in blood should be warm, and that being cold may actually be a sign of poor circulation. *Excess* heat is always a cause for concern in any hoof, but an even warmth in all four hooves can be a good sign. Thermography studies show that the shod hoof has a very different heat pattern compared to a barefoot hoof, and there is no gradual change in temperature throughout the capsule; it is much more abrupt.

A preliminary study performed by Duncan Mclaughlin and Easycare[7] demonstrated that the booted hoof will also only change in temperature by a few degrees, compared to the shod hoof, the temperature of which was raised by almost twice as much after a 50-mile ride. These findings could indicate inflammation of the hoof capsule, although further studies are scheduled to be carried out, to try to prove or disprove this theory.

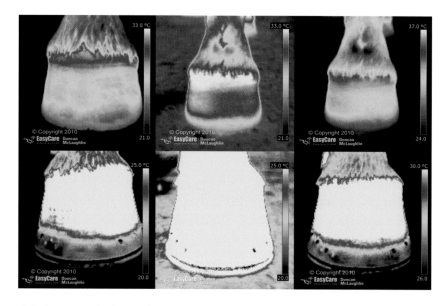

This thermography image shows the different heat patterns in shod and barefoot horses before, during and 30 minutes after exercise. The top images show a barefoot hoof that was booted during exercise (all images are taken of the naked hoof) and demonstrates how the bare hoof has a higher initial temperature (indicating better circulation) but very little rise during exercise compared to the shod hoof. The bare hoof also shows a gradual change in temperature across the hoof capsule, whereas the shod hoof shows an abrupt change.

Dr Robert Bowker DVM has done many studies into the differences in shod and unshod hooves, and one study gives a clear indication of the advantages of a bare or appropriately booted hoof (with pads, which are used inside the boots, beneath the horse's sole). He writes:

On softer surfaces (e.g. pea rock, sand or foam pads), blood flow will slow down and trickle through small vessels – microvenous vessels. On hard surfaces (e.g. cement or wood blocks), tissue perfusion dramatically decreases, so blood moves faster through the foot – it must stay in the large vessels. Different surfaces will change tissue perfusion, with softer, more forgiving surfaces having the greatest tissue perfusion.[8]

On hard surfaces such as roads, it can thus reasonably be argued that a hoof boot with a pad in is actually more beneficial that a bare hoof when riding for very long periods. Regarding shoes, a metal shoe that lifts the hoof off most surfaces exacerbates this circulation problem by causing peripheral loading, and Bowker's research explains how, in a shod hoof on a flat surface, blood flow actually comes to a halt for a split second with every heartbeat at the level of the horse's fetlock.

Lack of circulation can also play a part in bone degeneration, leading to conditions such as navicular syndrome and other degenerative diseases.

There is an old saying that 'horses have five hearts', owing to the pumping action of a bare hoof. However, with nailed-on shoes, because of the differences in blood profusion and circulation in the hoof, it is widely recognised that the horse's heart will have to work harder to push the blood down through the hoof and back up the leg. In a barefoot horse, the 'pump' mechanism of the hoof, being unimpeded, allows the horse's body to function correctly.

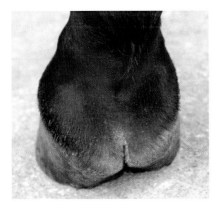

LEFT This photo shows a contracted heel and deep (owing to infection) central sulcus of a recently de-shod horse. Infection of the frog and white line are far more common in shod horses, where the circulation and stimulation issues prevent the hoof from being able to deal with them effectively unaided.

ABOVE A hoof boot that allows the hoof to function correctly means the hoof is still 'bare' within it. Boots can provide excellent protection on rough surfaces, and are only needed for a relatively short period compared to the time spent without boots in the paddock.

Traction

A naturally bare or booted hoof will almost always offer better traction on hard, flat surfaces such as roads than a shod hoof (with no additional studs or nails). On softer going, a bare hoof will cut into the ground to give good purchase, but the shod horse does have the advantage of being able to have studs put into the shoes to afford better purchase. It should also be noted, however, that hoof boots can also be studded. Studs can actually unbalance the hoof and can create a increased risk of injury (through joint or muscle/ligament damage), so they should be used sparingly: understud rather than overstud for the event is the rule – be it in shoes or boots.

Maintenance

Most owners report their horses become more confident and often even less spooky without shoes. The bare hoof gives the horse better feedback of the ground surface, which is very reassuring to a prey animal!

A shod horse will probably require less thought being given to the hooves between shoeings than a barefoot horse will (at least in the beginning): the latter needs the owner to be aware of the horse's feet at all times. A shod horse will be able to work on most surfaces with no conditioning, helped by the fact that the hoof capsule is often a little numb from the effect of the shoe. The barefoot horse may need to be conditioned to work on all surfaces comfortably, and boots may need to be applied in some cases for riding. One thing a lot of barefoot horse owners relish is being able to go and collect their horse from the field with no fear of finding they have cast a shoe, especially just before an event!

In conclusion, there are many physical reasons that can be given for a horse to be kept without shoes. Consideration must, however, be given to the amount of work this may or may not involve and whether the owner is prepared to be committed enough to see the horse through transition and beyond. For example, if a horse is constantly sore or lame because the owner is unwilling to make changes to the horse's lifestyle or use boots to keep the horse comfortable when required, it would have to be argued that they would be better to continue to shoe the horse than possibly cause the horse long-term discomfort. Discussing your options with a good hoof care practitioner is always the best way to help you to decide whether taking your horse barefoot is the best option for you and your horse.

References

6. The Strasser Controversy, A Guide for Newcomers to Barefoot by Yvonne Welz (reproduced with permission).

7. A preliminary study using infrared thermography by Duncan McLaughlin and Easycare Inc.

8. Bowker, R.M. 2003. Contrasting structural morphologies of 'good' and 'bad' footed horses, 49th American Association of Equine Practitioners Convention. 49: 186–209.

Chapter THREE

WHO SHOULD TRIM YOUR HORSE – AND WHAT METHODS WILL THEY USE?

ONE OF THE MOST IMPORTANT people you will need to work with when taking your horse barefoot is a good hoof care professional. This it the person who will be responsible for your horse's soundness (hoof-wise), as well as your biggest source of information about your individual horse's diet and maintenance needs. Thus, you need to feel confident in their methods.

Every horse (and owner) is different, and it can be confusing trying to decide whom you should trust to care for your horse's needs. One of the contentious issues in the hoof care world is that, unlike shoeing, where a farrier has a recognised qualification, it is not illegal for a non-farrier to trim a horse's hoof, as long as they are not preparing the hoof for a shoe. However, in 2010, in order to safeguard the horse's welfare and help protect the owner, LANTRA (the UK's Sector Skills Council for land-based and environmental industries) produced, with input from some of the recognised trimming associations in the UK, the National Occupational Standard (NOS) for Equine Barefoot Care.[9]

Under this professional standard, in order to call himself or herself a hoof care professional (if not already a registered farrier), an individual must be able to demonstrate skill and knowledge about their trade. Like all equine carers and/or practitioners, the individual is also bound by the animal welfare acts and business laws of the UK.

A good hoof care professional (HCP) is a highly trained and dedicated individual who is devoted to helping horses become and stay sound through natural hoof care. Nonetheless, one of the very best ways to find a suitable trimmer is through recommendation. As with farriery, the standard of hoof care professionals *can* vary, and you should do your research before employing anyone to care for your horse's feet, whatever their qualifications may be on paper.

A good trimmer will be more than happy to come and give you an initial consultation with your horse, giving you the opportunity to ask questions and understand what your horse will need to be a sound and happy barefoot horse. You need to feel you can communicate with them and ask them any questions, or tell them about any worries you have. Keep in mind that you are paying a professional for their opinion, but it is just that: there are plenty of other highly experienced people out there who may have a different but equally valid opinion of what is best for your horse, and you may feel more comfortable working with them. There are a few different hoof care associations in the UK (see next section), as well as a few very good independent trimmers, and you may feel more comfortable with one association's ideas than another's, or with a particular trimmer's attitude or personality.

The hoof is a structure that takes time to adapt, and you should be wary of anyone who promises 'perfect hooves' within a few weeks. Trimming is really a small part of the equation of healthy hooves, and invasive trimming that leaves a horse less sound than before the trim is just not acceptable. Movement is vital to the health of the hoof, and causing a horse to be sore is counterproductive to the healing and maintenance of the hooves. Since it takes time for the horse to grow better hooves you should be prepared to work with your HCP in the long term and to make alterations to diet and management where needed, to support the trim they will provide.

An explanation of trimming groups

There are a variety of groups and individuals operating in the UK; the groups with the most members in the UK are as follows.

Equine podiatrists

Equine podiatrists are represented by two groups in the UK; IAEP and EPAUK.

IAEP

The Institute of Applied Equine Podiatry (IAEP) was founded by K.C. La Pierre, RJF, MIAEP, Ph.D. The IAEP uses a trim known as the High Performance Trim method (HPT). As they explain:

> The HPT Method™ was developed in direct response to the Suspension Theory of Hoof Dynamics (La Pierre, 99). It is [K.C. La Pierre's] belief that this theory closest represents the true biomechanics of the hoof. As the theory was forming, it became increasingly apparent that how the hoof dissipated the energies produced during impact played an important role in keeping the horse sound. As with any object subject to kinetic energy (shock), its shape is what determines where the energies are directed, thus hoof conformation and how a trim was applied appeared to be of greatest importance.[10]

The HPT is not based on the wild horse model, but on a systematic, more 'mathematical' method that is said to be easy to understand and implement. K.C. La Pierre offers many books and DVDs on the details of his method, as well as a unique club, The Perfect Hoof Club.

EPAUK

The Equine Podiatry Association UK (EPAUK) was launched in April 2006 to exist as a self-regulating professional body for Equine Podiatrists practising in the UK. The website of the Equine Podiatry Association UK, or EPAUK, explains that their members are:

> Highly trained specialists in shoeless hoofcare who work closely with owners to achieve the healthiest hooves possible for their horse. Our approach is somewhat different to traditional farriery, educating owners so that they can understand how different factors influence the health of the hoof, helping to develop hoof-friendly horse management practices and providing close support and guidance as the horse's hooves change.
>
> It has been proven many times that the horse has the innate ability

to heal itself, and EPs (equine podiatrists) work hard to ensure that the maxim 'do no harm' is followed. Their hoofcare system is based on a very effective model which takes a complex structure (the equine foot) and breaks it down into a number of key parts that enable the EP to assess the health of your horse's feet and recommend ways of improving that health. An EP's most important tool is time, a tool which is utilised most effectively by the owner, who is expected to follow a personalised daily hoofcare routine which will improve the health of their horse's hooves.[11]

The AANHCP

The AANHCP (The Association for the Advancement of Natural Horse Care Practices), formerly known as the American Association of Natural Hoof Care Practitioners, was founded in the US by Jamie Jackson, a former farrier and one of the first proponents of natural horse-keeping and hoof care.

After studying wild horses for a number of years in the 1980s, Jamie became convinced that there was a better way to keep our own domestic horses and worked to develop a system of care for domestic horses that closely replicated how horses live in the wild. Early in the current century, he created the American Association of Natural Hoof Care Practitioners, a non-profit-making organisation devoted to education and training, giving people the option to complete a certification programme to become a Natural Hoof Care Practitioner. Since then, the organisation has expanded its scope and changed its name to the Association for the Advancement of Natural Horse Care Practices.

According to Jamie, the guiding principles to natural hoof care are:

1. Leave that which should be there naturally.

2. Take only that which would be worn away naturally in the wild.

3. Allow to grow that which should be there naturally, but is not due to unnatural forces.

4. Ignore all pathology.

The mission statement of the AANHCP is: 'To advance the humane care and management of domestic equines worldwide through the applications of proven practices and principles based on the research and findings of wild, free-roaming equines.' Jamie has written many books on the subject of barefoot and natural horse-keeping, including the highly regarded natural movement system known as 'paddock paradise'.

UKNHCP

UK Natural Hoof Care Practitioners (UKNHCP), was founded in 2006 as an organisation for professional hoof care practitioners focusing on whole horse health and improving barefoot horse performance.

The UKNHCP states that their four key objectives are:

1. To improve the health, welfare and quality of the life of horses in domestication.

2. To use current research and carry out research into hoof function and horse health.

3. To provide high quality training for all levels of the hoof care profession.

4. To share and demonstrate their findings and practical experience with the wider equine community.

The UKNHCP is not affiliated with the AANHCP.

Other groups

There are trimmers affiliated to other groups practising in the UK, including The Equine Science Academy and The American Hoof Association (AHA). As previously mentioned, there are also individuals who have come from either a more traditional farriery background, or have arrived through other studies.

What about Strasser?

The Strasser method is one that will no doubt be mentioned at some time when discussing barefoot hoof care – often as a caveat, as it was the 'Strasser trim' that was one of the first methods of barefoot hoof care outside of pasture trims seen in the UK.

The method used can be surgical in its nature, and hit the headlines during a welfare case a few years ago when this highly specialised trim was used. Dr Strasser now states that there is no such thing as 'the Strasser trim', and that she has merely copied the form of the healthy hoof that all horses are born with. She explains through her website and books how she has learned to replicate this on domestic horses, when they are not given the facilities to wear their hooves down naturally.[12]

The UK Strasser Hoofcare Organisation web page explains that:

> Dr Strassers' aim is to bring the concept of the correctly balanced hoof to the owner of the horse. Whether you decide to use a farrier or any other type of barefoot trim for your horse, you should be able to recognise a healthy hoof, and recognise problems in your horses' hooves. Most horse owners investigate other types of hoofcare when problems such as lameness, laminitis, navicular or stumbling have been going on for long periods of time, and their current equine professionals have not been able to effect any improvements. We suggest that your first response should be to educate yourself, then go back and discuss what you have learned with your current professionals.[13]

I feel that Dr Strasser has an undeniable place in barefoot history and that the research that Dr Strasser has given to the barefoot world should be viewed as valuable research of natural horse management and hoof care. I do not, however, advocate any method of maintaining the hooves that leave a horse less sound after a trim than before, so this is not a system I would recommend for maintaining your horse's hooves.

Can a farrier trim my barefoot horse?

A farrier should obviously be very capable of producing what would be referred to as a barefoot trim, but it is very much down to the individual farrier and how good their knowledge is on the subject; so do not presume that they will naturally be able to do it! The vast majority of the farriers' syllabus is based around shoeing/shod horses, metal working and preparing the foot for a shoe. At the time of writing, I am told that a specialist section on barefoot horses is being written, so that in the future, farriers should be better equipped but, at the moment, most farriers when de-shoeing a horse will carry out a pasture trim (see next section) which, in most cases, differs from what most barefoot-savvy people would recognise as a trim suitable for a working barefoot horse.

The other vital difference is that most traditional farriers are not taught to supply the information needed about diet, exercise and booting, which are factors that are so very important to the success of keeping a horse barefoot. There are some excellent farriers who are very willing to learn about this modern way of keeping horses without shoes, so if you already have a good farrier (who may even have suggested that you try your horse without shoes), do talk to them to see if this is something they have got the knowledge about, or are willing to learn. You will also find that some farriers will tell you that your horse cannot go barefoot, or that horses in general can't work without shoes – if this is the case, it would be sensible to get at least one other opinion (either from another farrier with a history of barefoot clients, or a good HCP), regarding your horse's ability to work without shoes before ruling out the barefoot option.

Pasture trim versus 'barefoot' trim

Different trimming schools base their methods on different ideals; for example, some are centred around the wild mustangs, and this method is known as the 'wild hoof model' the most famous advocate of this being Jamie Jackson of the AANHCP, who sticks absolutely to these ideals. This trim is based on a very minimalist trim to replicate the wear on the hooves of the wild herds in the USA. The other notable method used by Equine Podiatrists is a more mathematically based approach, using markers within the hoof (notably the HPT method developed by K.C. La Pierre). Both methods will usually produce a similar looking result on a healthy hoof. Some HCPs will sit in between the two methods, but in my opinion, the best trim is the one that suits that particular horse, no matter how it is achieved.

The pasture trim

So, what is so special about the trim a barefoot horse needs? There is a difference between the trim a farrier gives when preparing the foot for a metal shoe, and (in most cases) when performing a pasture trim. The pasture trim usually involves the farrier removing the dead sole and often

the toe callus, trimming/neatening the frog and then trimming the wall back level with the sole. Some farriers may, however, do the opposite with the wall, and leave a long rim of sole in the belief that it will keep the horse more comfortable.

The outer wall is not usually dressed more than a couple of millimetres (about $\frac{1}{16}$ in) to remove the sharp edges. Often, the sole is left unnaturally flat (if the wall is lowered in line with the pared sole) and the horse will often be slightly sore over stones or on flat surfaces for a few days or more (but usually sound at pasture), until he builds up a new layer of dead sole and insensitive frog to protect the sensitive tissues.

It is commonly seen that, with a pasture trim, the heels and/or toes are left a little longer than would be deemed to be a natural length too, which can affect gait and breakover.

ABOVE LEFT A pasture-trimmed hoof.

ABOVE RIGHT Sole of a pasture-trimmed hoof. Note the stretched white line, flat sole, wasted frog and uneven thickness of the hoof wall.

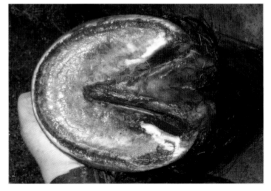

The same hoof as in the previous two photos, 3 months after professional care from Dawn Saunders, an AHA practitioner, shows much greater concavity, fuller frog, wider heels and a much tighter white line.

The barefoot trim

The trim a working barefoot horse requires is a bit different. There are obviously variations owing to the methods used by different trimming schools, and sometimes when treating pathology, but the basic maintenance trim on a healthy hoof should, whatever the methodology, produce a very similar result. The aim of a barefoot trim is for the horse to walk away from the trim moving as well as, or better, than he walked into it. In light of this, the sole may be cleaned of loose sole debris, but no hard sole is removed, and the frog will only be trimmed if there is diseased material – but never for cosmetic or routine purposes. The frog, like the sole, forms a hardened layer which, if removed, leaves more sensitive tissue that is more prone to pressure and infection. Thus, only what must be trimmed is trimmed.

This hoof shows flare, but demonstrates the 'healing angle', usually around an inch at the top, which is the angle at which the horse needs to grow the hoof.

The same hoof after a maintenance trim. Some flare has been removed, but taking the wall back any more would thin the outer wall, weakening it and leaving the horse more prone to injury from impact against the outer wall.

The hoof wall will be lowered around equally, to approximately 2mm (about $\frac{1}{16}$ in) inch above the solar plane, and is then bevelled back to the water line – the unpigmented horn between the outer wall and the white line (this practice is often known as the mustang roll). This rolled effect is one of the important differences between a barefoot and pasture trim, and will prevent chipping and control flaring, which are usually prevalent in pasture-trimmed hooves.

The other big difference is frequency – it is not unusual for a pasture-trimmed horse to go many weeks, or even 2–3 months between trims. Meanwhile, a working barefoot horse will be trimmed more regularly to

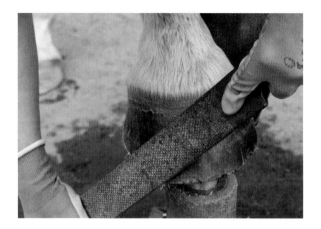

Dressing the outside wall is necessary to remove any flare, but should not be performed more than approximately one-third of the way up the hoof capsule to prevent overthinning/ weakening of the hoof capsule.

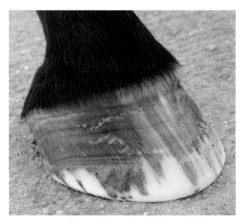

This hoof has had the excess growth removed and although only a light rasp was needed the hoof looks far more compact. This highlights the importance of small, regular trims, as the hoof capsule will react to any amount of overgrowth very quickly by changing the angle or slowing the rate of growth to compensate.

The heels are lowered individually to ensure correct balance. A bare hoof will usually have a naturally low heel.

ABOVE *This hoof is 4 weeks since trimming and the photo shows that a natural scoop at the quarters has developed. When the horse puts his full weight on this hoof at speed, the hoof capsule will expand and the quarters would become weight-bearing, especially on soft ground.*

RIGHT *Steven Leigh applying the bevel or mustang roll. A balance must be sought between enough of a roll to relieve the outer wall and prevent chipping and splitting (especially where flare is present, and at the toe), but without removing so much as to begin to weaken the hoof capsule, resulting in the hoof wearing too quickly on abrasive surfaces.*
(Photo DLT photography)

maintain this neat hoof capsule. Hooves respond to wear and, by allowing a hoof to grow long, it will encourage the slowing and changing of the angle of growth in an attempt to self-trim and regain frog/sole contact. A good barefoot trim is purely mimicking the wear patterns a horse would experience if he were allowed to roam freely across differing terrain. As mentioned earlier, domestic horses seldom cover enough miles over varied terrain to keep their hooves in optimum condition, and working on cambered roads can produce unnatural wear. Hence, a little human intervention is required in the form of a 'natural' trim.

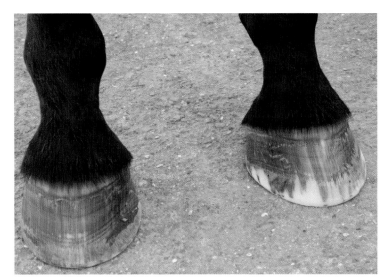

This horse has hooves that are very different from each other. It is important that the horse's conformation is taken into consideration when trimming the hooves, and that each hoof is treated as an individual that makes up a larger picture. Trying to correct hooves to make them 'match' can put strain on limbs that may also be different: a good trimmer will be able to identify when to respect the differences in the hooves.

Learning to maintain the rolled edge on your horse's hooves between professional trims is ideally done using one of the safe tools designed to prevent accidental removal of the wall. A quick run round the edge when you pick out the hooves every few days will often extend the time needed between professional trims, and help prevent any chipping or splitting from occurring.

References

9. www.lantra.co.uk/Downloads/Standards-qualifications/NOS/NOS-documents/ Equine-Barefoot-Care-NOS-(April-2010).aspx
10. www.appliedequinepodiatry.org/iaep/not_another_trim.html
11. www.epauk.org/aboutep.php
12. www.ukstrasserhoofcare.co.uk/content/
13. www.ukstrasserhoofcare.co.uk/content/

Chapter FOUR

TRANSITION – THE EARLY STAGES

THE TRANSITIONAL PERIOD occurs when a horse has had his shoes removed, and is in the process of getting accustomed to life without them. Usually, if there are no other problems, the best time to remove your horse's shoes is at the end of a shoeing cycle, when your horse is due to be shod again – this is when there will be the maximum wall length available to trim. Because of the trim required to fit a shoe, if the shoes are removed within the first couple of weeks, the horse will most likely be unusually sore, as the hoof has not been trimmed to cope without the shoe on and the wall may be abnormally short. You can use the time before the shoes are removed to make changes to the diet and maintenance of your horse, which should make transition even easier! If your horse already has a problem such as laminitis, this initial period of recovery should be seen as rehabilitation and not transition, as it is not just the after-effects of the metal shoe you have to contend with.

The transition from being shod to going barefoot depends on many factors. How long and how well the horse has been trimmed and shod, how good his diet was, how much exercise he has been given/allowed, as well as things we are less in control of such as genetics and past or present injuries, all contribute to the soundness of the hoof you are removing the shoe from. When taking a horse barefoot, you are suddenly allowing the hoof to function to full capacity, which includes greatly improving the circulatory system and the firing of nerves. This will, in turn, bring to light the true state of health in a newly de-shod hoof, which can manifest itself in the form of soreness and lameness during the transitional phase. Some people will say that, if a horse is not immediately sound without shoes, then that horse will not cope with being barefoot. However, if the horse is not happy without shoes, it has to be questioned whether that horse is clinically sound; to my mind, if a horse needs a piece of metal nailed to a hoof to keep him sound, it indicates issues within the hoof, and the horse would therefore benefit from removing it and allowing the hoof to recover!

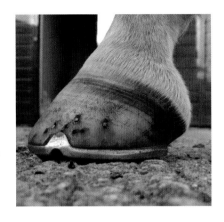

A hoof that would be described as well shod; the shoe fits the hoof nicely and the hoof is well trimmed, but the effects of the shoe are obvious in the under-run heels and horn weakened with nail holes.

The early days

When the shoes are initially removed, a horse that has no major issues and has been regularly well balanced and shod will usually be sound immediately at pasture, and is often sound for at least short distances on a hard, flat surface and only sore on uneven or stony, hard surfaces. With this horse you could expect to complete much of the transition in a few weeks (under the right conditions), whereas a horse that has very flat soles and has been shod with flare will probably take a good few months to get to the same level of comfort.

ABOBVE The newly de-shod hoof shows the common problems of a flat sole with a build-up of dead horn unable to wear away naturally, and a stretched white line with signs of mild infection with white line disease.

LEFT The characteristically flat sole and weak horn of a horse that has been shod for many years – this horse's shoes were removed 2 weeks before this photo was taken. This horse went on to be trimmed and maintained in the barefoot way shortly after!

You can get an idea if you think back to when your horse lost a shoe – did it bother him? Did he go instantly sore on the foot, or did you finish what you were doing and notice it on the way back home? Even if your horse does seem fine straight away without shoes, you do need to bear in mind that there are a lot of physical changes taking place in the hoof that you can't see, and it is easy to inadvertently cause soreness if you do too much too soon.

Hoof growth is stimulated by movement and wear; it is a reactive process, so the hooves need to be given time to respond to the increased requirements placed on them. If, for example, you took your newly bare-foot (but reasonably fit) horse out and did the same amount of roadwork as he was used to in the first few weeks, with no build-up and without using hoof boots with pads, you would almost certainly run into a situation where the horse's natural hoof growth was not keeping up with the wear, and the hooves would start to show signs soreness and a 'lack of growth'. Imbalances or changes in gait might also start to creep in.

Almost certainly, a horse coming out of shoes will initially have a long hoof capsule and a thin sole, and the hoof may well be lacking concavity.

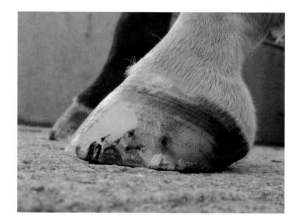

The newly de-shod hoof will be more prone to chips and cracks until the nail holes have grown out, as they act as sites prone to infection. It is also possible for newly de-shod horses to suffer from one or more abscesses (particularly if they have been in shoes for many years, or poorly shod with great restriction to the circulation). This should not be a particular cause for concern but, of course, should be treated appropriately.

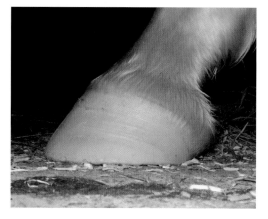

The same hoof as in the adjacent photo, after a few months of a good diet, plenty of movement and correct, regular trimming. No infection, no bruising, just a beautiful looking and very practical hoof!

Because of the peripheral loading the shoe enforces on the foot (which occurs when the weight of the horse is taken on the outer wall), the sole, frog and heel are not always given the stimulus that they should have, and this leads to the internal structures becoming slacker and often less well developed. This is especially true if the horse is shod before the age of 5, while these structures are developing. Movement is crucial to the transitional phase, and boots and pads should be used to enable the horse to keep working during this phase if needed. This will also prevent a drop in the horse's fitness, enabling no break in the rider's plans either – so the rider is happy and the horse's hooves benefit from the added stimulation at the same time! The key during this phase is to listen to your horse and do whatever you need to keep him sound and comfortable whilst waiting for his hooves to adapt to the new stimulation.

Initial sensitivity

It is also widely accepted that shoes cause a big impact on circulation, and some research suggests that nerves are compressed and damaged while shoes are worn – so having the shoes removed and the subsequent return of sensation can be a lot for the hoof (and horse!) to cope with at first. It is sometimes compared to the feeling you experience when you have lain on your arm

ABOVE *Your horse may be sensitive to walking on uneven or stony ground when first without shoes but, with time and the use of boots and pads to protect and condition him, he will soon be able to tackle any surface, like this competitive driving pony.*

LEFT *A stretched white line is common amongst newly de-shod horses, and special attention needs to be paid as small stones and grit can become lodged and cause infection in the beginning. Using hoof boots when riding on gravel is a good way to prevent this until the white line has tightened up.*

at night and it has gone 'dead'; it can be quite uncomfortable while the nerve endings regain feeling. If this is similar to how horses feel, even to a lesser degree, it is no surprise they can look a little sore for a short while at first! This initial sensitivity can be greatly improved by the use of hoof boots with appropriate pads to cushion and support the hoof. The boots will protect the newly sensitive sole and provide comfort, to the point where most horses will move at least as well as (and in most cases better than) when shod, immediately the padded boots are put on.

Preparation is key

Talk to your hoof care professional before you remove the shoes, so you can get a rough idea of timescale and what you can expect for your individual horse. However good your horse's feet are before the shoes are removed, it is a good idea to get his diet checked and changed if necessary, so he has all the nutrients needed to start growing the 'new hooves' from the moment the shoes are taken off.

The other essential thing to consider during the transition is how to keep the horse moving. It cannot be underestimated how important movement is to the health of a horse's hoof. Stimulation is one of the major factors that determine hoof growth and quality. In some extreme cases it may be necessary to restrict exercise (for example, a horse at the start of laminitis with a currently unstable pedal bone), but pretty much all other horses will benefit far more from as much exercise as you want to give them (within the realms of their fitness level), along with 24/7 turnout in a suitable area. This, as mentioned earlier, is where the use of hoof boots becomes so important, as they will allow your horse to make the transition without discomfort, whilst allowing you to continue to ride and enjoy your horse, in the knowledge that you are helping him to grow better hooves at the same time!

Some hoof care practitioners (although a minority) dislike hoof boots and will tell you there is no need for them, or they see them as 'artificial', or not truly barefoot. They feel it is better to make the transition in horses by walking them over rough surfaces, often with the horses feeling at least occasional discomfort day-in, day-out until their hooves begin to react and become tough enough to cope. Consistency is no doubt important, and this method will work eventually in most cases if everything else is correct;

but it can take a long time, and the rider is usually grounded. I also question this method as it does cause the horse some level of discomfort, and he is unable to do as much exercise as usual, which is counterproductive.

With the advent of modern boots there is, to my mind, no excuse not to use them, if your horse needs them. Barefoot advocate and farrier Pete Ramey admits in his excellent DVD series 'Under The Horse' that a good few years ago, he used only to recommend boots to clients whose horses were still struggling after a couple of months, and felt defeated if he had to suggest them. However, he quickly discovered that by using pads (which he designed in conjunction with manufacturer Easycare) within the boots, he could achieve transition in a horse faster, without a single lame step. He now has a policy of only removing a horse's shoes if the client is prepared to buy boots and pads at the time.

Abscesses – a common problem

Although most horses will sail through the transitional period without a concern if boots are used when needed, there *can* be issues that pop up along the way. One of the most common problems is abscesses so, if your horse develops sudden severe lameness (within a matter of hours sometimes), which can be quite unnerving, try not to panic; it is most probably an abscess developing! Nevertheless, best practice is to consult your vet for a diagnosis and some management advice, and to rule out more serious conditions.

Horses that have been badly shod, or have been shod for a long period of their life, are far the most likely to develop one or more abscesses during the transitional period, so it is not a given that all horses will develop them. The reason why they develop is the sudden improvement in circulation once the shoes are removed. The lack of circulation in the shod foot causes an accumulation of cellular debris within the hoof capsule. When the shoes come off, the circulation is restored and the body can finally get to work removing the accumulated material. Unfortunately, some of this accumulation is not easily absorbed into the bloodstream, so the only way for the body to expel the debris is by forming an abscess.

If you suspect your horse is developing an abscess, it is sensible to have a chat to your HCP and keep in touch with them. If the horse does have an abscess and it breaks out quickly by itself, it will usually do so through the coronet band or the heel – anywhere there is soft tissue. If this happens, you need to ensure the area is kept clean, and poulticing is a useful way to help drain the area more quickly. Boot the horse up and allow him to move as much as he wants to, as the more he moves around, the quicker the body can expel the waste and heal itself. If there is no sign of an exit hole and the horse is very lame, it is advisable to talk to your vet or HCP to see if they feel it should be drained manually. There are quite different schools of thought about the treatment; the traditional method is to effect a hole for the pus to release from (as long as the abscess is not too deep within the hoof), and this will give immediate relief. However, it will leave the hoof compromised where the hole has been created, so some HCPs will

advise allowing the process to run its course and exit where the body wants it to. Either way, it is a sensible precaution to make sure that you have knowledgeable help on hand, and usually within a few days of identifying the problem, your horse will be firmly back on track towards having a set of strong, healthy hooves!

The end result of a successful transition under the watchful eye of a knowledgeable trimmer: this hoof belongs to a horse that had just completed a 17-mile ride completely barefoot over greatly differing terrain.

Chapter FIVE

DIETARY REQUIREMENTS OF THE BAREFOOT HORSE

NUTRITION IS A VERY IMPORTANT part of hoof care, and yet it is something frequently misunderstood, not only by horse owners, but also by some farriers. Modern hoof care professionals (including farriers who specialise in barefoot horses) will place great emphasis on diet, and will take the time to discuss the subject with you and help you decide what is appropriate for your horse or pony.

Trim

Diet   Exercise

The barefoot pyramid of success. Get the foundations right, and your trim will have a solid base and your horse will have rock-crunching hooves!

As with any animal, what you put into the body influences how well the body can function, and how healthy the animal is. When there are imbalances, illness is more likely, and even life-expectancy can be reduced. Today, there is an increasing amount of published information and a general awareness about the consequences of the food we eat; for example, the need to eat our '5 a day' to stay healthy. Our horses are no different!

Usually, a healthy barefoot horse doesn't require a 'special' kind of diet, just one that is appropriate and as close to natural as possible. Unfortunately, it is very common for horses to be kept on a pretty unnatural diet, and this is no doubt a contributing factor to the number of horses (both shod and unshod) that have supposedly poor hooves, as well as other health problems including allergies and skin conditions. The difference a diet can make to a hoof (and the rest of a horse!) is quite incredible and, in as little as a few weeks, you will begin to see a marked improvement in your horse's hooves, once a poor diet is rectified.

Nutrition is a complex subject, and every horse should be treated as an individual. Whole books are written on the subject, and I would always recommend that you seek advice from a good hoof care professional or nutritionist about your horse's personal circumstances, if you have particular concerns.

Natural versus 'domesticated' diet

Horses are naturally grazers and browsers, and will travel many miles every day in order to satisfy their need for food. Their bodies have evolved to work at their optimum on a constant trickle of fibre through the gut, and the constant movement helps to ensure efficient digestion. In the wild, they would be eating mainly dry or short grasses, in addition to herbs, hedges and trees where available. However, a traditionally kept, domesticated horse is usually confined in a small field of only a few acres (less, in many cases), or is stabled. The fields are planted with hardy grasses (with no herbs), and are fertilised to ensure the grass is green and grows strongly for as much of the year as is possible, which results in a much higher sugar and starch content, and much easier pickings.

Grass in one form or other will make up the bulk of the barefoot horse's diet.

Hay is generally fed only when grass is in short supply, and usually in limited quantities, so there are periods when the horse has nothing to eat. Hard feed is commonly given twice a day, and usually contains a mixture of cereals, often coated in molasses to reduce dust and make the feed more appetising.

On the surface, you may think there is not a huge difference between the 'natural' diet and that of a traditionally kept, domesticated horse. After all, the horse is still eating grass, but with a few extras on top – right? However, when you delve a bit deeper, you can start to appreciate just how far from nature we have taken our horses. A horse's diet is naturally fibre-based; without fibre the horse's gut cannot function properly. With a constant trickle of fibre through the gut, with occasional small amounts of herbs and other forage, the horse maintains a pretty steady level of sugar in the blood, and has a constant slow-burn energy source. However, many domestic horses are, as mentioned, fed a diet much higher in starch and sugar. This is likely to come not just from the fertilised grass, but from the regular addition of hard feeds, commonly supplied to give our horses extra energy, which very often is only needed to make up for the lack of slow-burn energy already missing in the diet. Ironically, more often than not, we then have to restrict grazing as the horse gains weight too easily – which then means periods with no food to eat, in contradiction to the horse's natural regime.

Benefits of a natural diet

Hooves (like our human nails) are a very telling indicator of the quality of the diet, and horses, just like humans, have different tolerances to levels of sugar and starch. Some horses can do well on a less-than-ideal diet and still have the quality of hoof you need to work them without shoes. These horses are usually in a good amount of work, so the food they eat is being burnt off and they are maintaining a good weight very easily – the effects of the higher starch and sugar are less obvious. Most horses, however, do need to keep to as natural a diet as possible, and there are many easy ways to make little improvements that will make a huge difference to hoof quality and overall horse health.

With the right nutrition and care Thoroughbred horses can grow a strong, sound hoof capsule just like any other horse!

Access to forage

Not fertilising the pasture is one such way; allowing pasture to regenerate naturally and using a broad meadow seed mix containing herbs and grasses instead of a traditional ryegrass mix. It is said that very long, rough-looking grass is far lower in sugar than very short-cropped grass as the short grass is 'stressed' and more likely to contain higher levels of sugar. This long, hay-like grass will also make sure the horse will not go without fibre for any length of time; however, where only short grass is available, piles of meadow hay left ad lib is another good option. If some form of track system (a form of 'movement management' – see Chapter 6 for more information) is being used within the field, this will allow more forage to be fed freely without fear of making the horse overweight. But where it is not possible to have a system to encourage movement, a few small-holed haynets dotted around the field to encourage some movement and slow the intake of food to a slow trickle will make a positive difference.

Horses that are laminitis-prone, insulin-resistant, or have any kind of metabolic disorder, usually do well with grass kept to an absolute minimum (or none at all) and, ideally, should to be fed soaked hay. Soaking hay in most cases reduces the sugar content to levels that are more acceptable for such horses. For most horses, choosing good-quality meadow hay (preferably organic and pesticide-free) over higher-protein hays such as lucerne or ryegrass will better suit the animal's digestion and metabolism. It should be noted that a minority of hoof care professionals advocate that no grass should be fed to any horse. This is because it is difficult to monitor the intake of the sugars present in grass; naturally, these individuals advocate turning the horse out for exercise onto grass-free pastures, and feeding grass-replacement forages. However, most feel that it is not always realistic to stick to such a rigid grass-free diet and still provide adequate turnout. Also, a hay-only diet can lead to deficiencies of certain minerals and omega-3 fatty acids that are often lacking in dried forage, so care should be taken if no fresh forage is offered.

Supplementation

Supplementation does not, in most instances, mean adding something 'unnatural' to the diet, but ensuring that a substance that is naturally required is present in sufficient quantity.

As we have seen, good-quality, low-sugar forage should form by far the largest part of a horse's diet. However, when relying on forage to supply everything your horse requires, it is important to make sure he is still receiving all the vitamins and minerals he needs to thrive, as a deficiency or imbalance will quickly show up in his hooves or general health. The simplest way to feed a horse with no particular additional energy requirements is to have your grass and hay analysed, and to supplement accordingly. Every part of the country will tend to be rich in, or lacking in, certain minerals, which can then be added to balance the diet very cost-effectively. If you do this, you will also be safe in the knowledge that you are not over-supplementing (see below). The other alternative is to use a broad-spectrum vitamin and mineral supplement (take care to choose one without added sugars!), in order to cover the possible imbalances. While this will probably be satisfactory in most cases, it is less precise, because the formulation is based on 'average' requirements.

Whichever way you choose to feed your horse, be it the scientific method of analysing and supplementing, or the more intuitive and experimental way of 'covering all bases', do be very sure that you are not

Supplements useful in a barefoot horse's diet include oil, ideally high in omega-3. Seaweed is recommended by many IICPs as it provides many micronutrients, in this case it is combined with rosehip, which is naturally high in biotin, a key nutrient in hoof and hair growth. Magnesium is often lacking in diets, especially in wet areas, and can make a huge difference to a 'footy' horse. Both prebiotics and probiotics (such as yeast) will aid digestion and help prevent gastric problems.

over-supplementing with any one vitamin or mineral. If, for example, you decide to feed a broad-spectrum supplement and a specialist hoof supplement, you would need to check that the two (along with the horse's bucket feed, if you are giving one) are not going to be supplying too much of a given mineral, as some can cause toxicity in excess, if the body is not able to expel them. Choose one reputable supplier, and stick to what they recommend, so you can be sure you are not over-supplementing, but are fulfilling your horse's nutritional needs.

That said, there are some vitamins and minerals that can be beneficial and fed safely in quantities that are larger than would occur naturally; these are often recommended for horses with persistent hoof issues, during the transition from shod to barefoot, or if there are other health issues such as laminitis to consider. Biotin (vitamin H) is one of the most well-known vitamins to promote hoof quality, and should ideally be fed in conjunction with methionine and often zinc, to aid absorption. However, one of the most significant elements in improving poor hoof quality appears to be magnesium. A heavy magnesium oxide supplement is often recommended by hoof care professionals for horses going barefoot, or horses that are 'footy' or laminitic, and is a very useful thing to try if hoof quality is not what it should be – even after all the changes have been made to the horse's diet and management regime.

Magnesium is also important for horses living in very wet areas, because rain and wet soil act to leach the magnesium out and, in horses generally, for the muscles and the nervous system – a jittery or spooky horse or one that 'ties up' (experiences severe muscle problems after work) could be a candidate for checking magnesium levels in the diet. When supplementing magnesium, it is important that it remains in correct ratio with other minerals, especially calcium (the dietary calcium (ca): magnesium (mg) ratio should be 2:1), and some sources say that the manner in which it is provided (i.e. the compound form) is important, both to ensure good-value efficacy and to avoid possible toxicity. Always choose a high-quality magnesium supplement and do seek the advice of a nutritional expert or your supplement company helpline if you are concerned about ratio and dosage.

One supplement I feel should be considered, whatever approach to feeding you take, is the provision of a good prebiotic and probiotic. *Probiotics* are live bacteria that have a beneficial effect on gut health and digestion.

A probiotic supplement contains a range of microorganisms that would be found naturally in the horse's gut. *Prebiotics* are short chains of simple sugars, glucose and fructose that cannot be digested in the small intestine – they are utilised entirely in the hindgut, and 'feed' the beneficial micro-flora, maintaining a stable gut environment. Adding prebiotics and pro-biotics serves as a very good nutritional insurance policy, and will ensure that your horse maintains a healthy gut and that the food he is eating is used to full benefit. I also feel that, as hoof-related problems such as laminitis can start in the gut, anything that will keep the gut in peak con-dition has to be worthwhile adding to the diet!

Ad lib salt should also be readily available, ideally loose and in block form, as this important electrolyte is something the horse will seek to balance himself.

'Short' feeds

If you do need to give bucket feed, perhaps to mix in supplements, or in order to keep your horses in a routine and allow you to check on them easily, stick to high-fibre, lower sugar and starch feeds. These include good-quality unmolassed sugar beet pulp, grass pellets or a ready prepared feed by a specialist manufacturer. More companies are starting to realise the importance of low starch and sugar in the horse's diet, quite aside from the barefoot angle, so the choice is becoming better every day. Small specialist manufacturers such as Thunderbrook Feeds, the Pure Feed Company and Simple Systems produce feeds aimed to meet the needs of barefoot horses, whilst forward-thinking companies such as Allen & Page are producing more fibre-orientated feeds, such as Fast Fibre.

There is, however, a debate about the suitability of some commonly used feedstuffs for horses; for example, some feed companies are con-cerned about the levels of pesticides and binding agents going into horse feeds, since, as with humans, these additives can cause a reaction in some individuals.

If your horse is in hard work, and really does need extra energy, beyond that supplied by good forage, there are ways of providing it without resort-ing to traditional grains. (Although always increase the workload before the feed, to avoid overfeeding!)

Alfalfa is a good source of protein, and can be fed at up to around 20 per cent of the horse's total forage intake if the alfalfa is being fed for its energy-giving purposes, but care must be taken not to cause a mineral imbalance when feeding this legume in any great quantity, as alfalfa has a high calcium to phosphorus ratio; commonly 3:1–5:1. Horses require twice as much calcium as phosphorus in the diet, or a 2:1 calcium (ca) to phos-phorus (p) ratio. Most hays have a ca:p ratio of 2:1.

Being a good source of 'calories' makes alfalfa ideal for horses working hard, but it is not a good choice for horses that are overweight!

Grains such as oats should be looked at more as a supplement than a staple, and it is not generally recommended to feed more than around 1 lb or so (about 0.5kg) a day, as they are liable to upset the horse's digestion and cause 'sugar spikes' (which is when a large amount of glucose enters the bloodstream). There is an idea that sprouting the grains before feeding helps to make them more digestible and more nutritionally correct for the horse, but not all groups agree that this is the case, so I feel that grain in general is best avoided whenever possible.

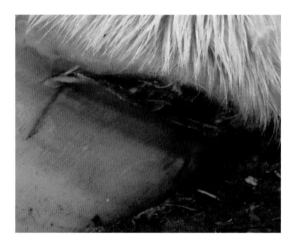

An injury to the coronet band can be very serious, but good nutrition, movement and regular barefoot trimming allowed this horse to recover fully with almost no sign of injury a year later. A similar injury on a shod horse could well have resulted in a permanent crack owing to the lack of circulation to heal the coronet band.

Chapter SIX

MANAGEMENT – THE IMPORTANCE OF MOVEMENT

WHEN I LOOK AT THE MANAGEMENT of barefoot horses, I think of it as a pyramid (see page 47). At the top is the trim, the bit everyone thinks of when they think 'barefoot horse'. Supporting this are the other two vital elements, diet (which we covered in the previous chapter) and movement. These foundations are what allow the horse to grow a hoof that is strong enough to *be* trimmed; without the foundations in place, the pyramid would topple. However, more than a few owners are happy to allow their horses just a couple of hours turnout a day, and feel this is a sensible precaution against injury and lameness.

When you remove the horse's shoes, you no longer have a metal frame to desensitise the hoof and mask the problems that lack of movement cause. Barefoot horses are 'honest' horses; they have the ability to feel everything as they should, and their hooves are a window to their general health. Good hooves can only be grown by a healthy body – just as it is said that a person's nails are an indicator of their own health.

Horses have evolved to roam many miles a day. Most estimates put this figure at around 20–30 miles per day, and this roaming across differing terrain is necessary to search for food, water and shelter. Domestic horses have no need to travel to find these basic needs; they have everything provided for them, so this requirement to roam is eliminated. However,

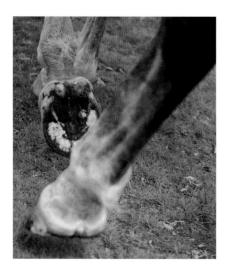

evolution is a slow process and the horse's hooves (and body) do still require a certain degree of exercise to keep healthy, just like the human body. Exercise can come in many forms, and the wonderful thing about a barefoot horse is that the miles you cover are not going to be adding anywhere near the stress on the horse's body that they would were he shod. This is because of the dramatic reduction in concussion and stress on the joints.

Every step the horse takes stimulates growth and improves circulation; the more you can encourage your horse to move through turnout and ridden work, the better his hooves will become!

Providing the opportunity for exercise

If you were lucky enough to have the time to ride for a good many miles a day, your horse's hooves would respond by becoming harder, growing faster and having a greater concavity than ever before. In the real world, however, most owners have jobs and other responsibilities that may limit the amount of time they can spend with their horses. It may not be possible to ride consistently from one week to the next, and there may be periods when the horse is not able to be ridden at all. It therefore makes sense to try to provide the horse with as much opportunity to exercise himself as possible.

Track systems

One of the easiest ways to provide more daily exercise for your horse is through turnout. Ideally, barefoot horses should be kept out at pasture 24/7, with good shelter, water and forage available. The pasture would ideally be arranged into a track system, often known as 'paddock paradise' and first written about extensively by Jamie Jackson some years ago. These tracks should vary in width, but always be wide enough to allow the horses contained within the system to pass each other safely (opinions vary, but for a small, amiable group of horses, 10ft minimum seems to work well). In this ideal, the aim of the track is to encourage the horses to travel along

A track system or paddock paradise is widely accepted to be the ideal way to keep a barefoot horse. Wide, bare tracks with hay, feed and water placed at intervals along the way will encourage movement and simulate the way a horse in the wild would move during the day.

paths, just as it has been observed that horses do in the wild. The longer you can make the track the better, and along this track there should be wider areas to allow the horses to play, shelter under a patch of trees, or drink, for example. Along this track, there would be varying gradients and surfaces and areas of pea gravel, especially around flooded watering holes to give the hooves moisture and stimulation. Rocky areas and sand also contribute to the environment the horses roam within, and benefit the natural wear of the hooves. The grass should be sparse and not fertilised or lush, so the horses have to travel to graze. Hay should be a good source of their diet and this should be distributed around the track, to further encourage movement. A circular track will usually work better than a straight one, as it will encourage a more natural movement pattern.

LEFT A flooded area within the paddock (around the water trough or anywhere the horse will have to walk for short periods) will ensure the hoof capsule maintains an ideal moisture balance.

ABOVE Different surfaces will help to produce a stronger hoof capsule and condition your horse for any surface he will meet out on a ride.

This method of keeping horses will undoubtedly create a wonderful environment for not only the hooves, but the whole horse to flourish in, but unfortunately the financial cost is usually prohibitive for most horse owners. In the UK, there are other factors that make it harder to set up, including planning restraints and a lack of land – these lead to more horses being in small yards with less land than in the USA, for example. Another major obstacle in the UK is the notoriously wet weather; narrow tracks with sparse grass growth can quickly become a boggy mess if no drainage is put in place!

However, despite these constraints I do firmly believe that any kind of track is of benefit, so even using electric fencing to zigzag back and forth across the field to encourage movement could considerably increase the distance the horse travels in a day. If you have your own land, another simple idea is to erect an electric fence around the inside perimeter to create a track of various widths, with the space in the middle available to cut for your own hay, if you so desire. The essence is, the further you can get from the basic square field where the horse has to travel minimum distance for maximum reward, the better.

Pea gravel is one of the best surfaces to include in any paddock system for barefoot horses as it will condition and gently wear a hoof. In studies pea gravel was shown to promote blood flow more than any other surface hence stimulating growth and repair within the hoof.

To include varying surfaces in a practical and economical way, spreading pea gravel (or, if unavailable, larger stones) in gateways, aprons and around water containers will give an alternative surface for the horses to travel across, and will help to combat mud at the same time. Note that products such as road planing (the material removed from the reconstruction of asphalt roads) are not recommended, as the tar and chemicals can stick to or penetrate the hooves and cause problems – which is, of course, counterproductive!

Whatever else is provided, good shelter and a clean water supply are obviously essential, and somewhere the horses can stand out of the mud to allow their feet to dry as required should also been seen as a necessity.

A horse kept on soft ground with no stone areas will develop a hoof adapted to that environment. This hoof shows the bars are laid over, not a necessarily a problem for this horse and easily trimmed by hand to replicate the natural wear but something that would be less likely to occur in a field with natural stone areas.

Shelter and fresh water are vital; gradients and plenty of relief from the mud also benefit the barefoot horse.

Can you keep your liveried horse barefoot?

But what if you have to keep your horse at a yard with restricted turnout; does that mean you cannot take your horse barefoot? Not at all! There are certain difficulties you will need to overcome, but there are many instances of barefoot horses with excellent hooves being stabled at least some of the time. If the fields are very wet, it actually has to be considered whether the horse is better stabled at night to allow them to dry (although the ideal would be a large barn in which horses can move freely together, as this would allow more natural equine behaviour, and far greater activity).

Mentally, horses are almost certainly happier when kept in a herd and in an environment where they can choose to move if they want to. As horses are travelling herd and prey animals, being stabled causes all sorts of potential problems, from the boredom of being confined, to the stiffness arising from lack of movement. However, a lot of horses appear to accept it, and if there is really no alternative, it is entirely possible for a fully stabled horse to be a barefoot horse too, with a few compromises.

The success of the stabled 'barefooter' will owe much to the amount of exercise received, and the cleanliness of the bed. Stable waste products (the horse's urine and faeces) will damage the horse's hooves, also making them soft and predisposed to infections such as thrush and white line disease. The stable needs to have a deep, absorbent bed that is cleaned regularly to ensure that the horse spends as little time as possible in contact with his own waste.

Also, and very importantly, the horse should be given as much exercise as possible; for example, being ridden, lunged and walked on a horse-walker – anything to keep the hooves working. It is possible that the stabled horse will always need hoof boots for ridden work outside the school, especially on uneven ground. This is especially true if most of the horse's work is performed on an artificial surface, as the hooves will condition to the surface they are used on. The benefits of barefoot are just as great for stabled horses; a shod horse with the added restriction of a stable will have worryingly little movement stimulation to encourage circulation in the hoof; the barefoot horse will have the benefit of unhindered blood flow, and a natural hoof capsule to support him. After all, which would you prefer, to stand all day in metal-soled shoes, or in bare feet?

Chapter SEVEN

THE BENEFITS OF HOOF BOOTS

I F YOU DECIDE TO TAKE YOUR horse barefoot, you would be forgiven for wondering whether hoof boots are so important; and why, having just removed the shoes, you are promptly covering the hooves back up again! It has certainly been argued by owners of shod horse that horses wearing hoof boots (either occasionally or regularly when working or competing) cannot be deemed to be 'barefoot', as their hooves are not truly bare. However, owners of barefoot horses and most hoof care professionals explain that 'barefoot' has become, for most people, a term to describe a method of keeping horses without the use of permanent shoes (be they nailed or glued on with inflexible adhesive). A horse that is booted for one or two hours a day has all the advantages of modern hoof protection when necessary, but the vast majority of the horse's life is spent without anything covering the hooves. Even when booted (in correctly fitting boots), hoof function is not affected as it is in metal shoes, so the hoof is still 'bare' insofar as the horse's body and the hoof function are concerned.

In years past, the only options were to nail metal shoes on, or leave your horse's hooves without protection. We now have the luxury of being able to offer our horses' hooves the best possible protection if needed, which has allowed many more horses than ever before to benefit from natural hoof care, should their owners wish it. In fact, hoof boots can actually be an advantage, especially to competition horses, and give the edge over their shod counterparts, in some situations. This is because a hoof boot gives the horse good traction, dramatically less concussion than a nailed-on metal shoe and complete sole protection; you will often see barefoot endurance horses cantering up stone-covered tracks where shod horses can only walk owing to the risk of damage to their exposed soles.

There are now boots to fit almost every shape and size of horse. Elizabeth Hill rode 1,300 miles around Britain in 2011 with her horses in hoof boots, attracting a lot of attention on the way!

Making compromises

In an ideal world, horses would not need to use hoof boots at all, but many factors, as already discussed, affect hoof quality and the reality for most horse owners wanting to keep their horses as naturally as possible is such that there will be compromises somewhere in the management. The most common problem is not being able to exercise the horse enough to fully condition the hooves. In order to condition a horse to be able to travel across a given surface, you need to be able to work him consistently on that type of ground. Many horse owners are not able to work their horses for increasing amounts of time every day across a multitude of surfaces, gradually building up the hooves' ability to cope with any surface.

As hooves are reactionary, riding a few times a week will, in many cases, never be enough to condition them to be 100 per cent on rough and stony ground. Another problem is that you may not have rough surfaces near where you ride or train, but wish to attend events further afield, where the ground conditions are rougher than at home, or are unknown. In either case, boots will give you the solution to enable your horse to do whatever you want with him without concern. It should, at this point, be noted that if you are planning to do a long or hard ride in the boots, just as you build the horse up fitness-wise, you should also allow the horse to become accustomed to the boots, both in terms of feel and weight. I have yet to come across a horse that will not wear boots; in some cases, once the horse has taken a few steps and realises the comfort they afford, he may even appear to be eager to get them on in future!

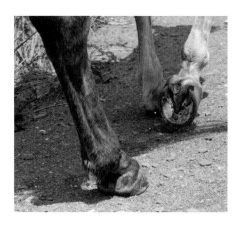

It can take time to condition a horse to be comfortable on any surface: boots with pads will allow your horse to stay completely comfortable whilst developing those rock-crunching feet every barefooter aspires to.

Hoof boots are useful in other ways too; they are fitted by owners of shod horses when the horse has an abscess, or needs protection and support during times of illness, such as laminitis. Some boots can even be used over a metal shoe to protect the horse's sole or afford more grip, but the primary reason for their production is to give owners an easy-to-use, modern alternative to nailed-on metal shoes, using high-tech, modern materials.

The history of hoof boots

Boots of various descriptions have been around for 40 years or more; one of the first and most notable being the Easyboot invented by Dr Neel Glass, a nuclear physicist at the Los Alamos Scientific Laboratory in New Mexico. The horse he and his wife had purchased for his daughters was diagnosed with navicular disease, and conventional shoeing with heel wedges was not helping. Dr Glass found the horse was much better without the restriction and shock of steel shoes, so began training as a farrier, and went about designing a hoof protection boot. (At this point I should interject that it is widely acknowledged that metal is not the best material to provide grip and shock-absorption. I have never seen a hoof boot with metal on the sole – other than fastenings – as there are far better materials for the job to be found, such as those used in athletics shoes, and even tyres!) Dr Glass began testing prototypes, and by the end of 1971 had patents in place for the pattern. He then went on to fit more of his horses in boots

Dr Neel Glass was one of the first pioneers of booting horses after his daughter's pony developed navicular disease. The inventor of one of the very earliest hoof boots made a mark on the horse world when he rode his horse in the Pony Express Race in 1979.

and competed them in some of the most gruelling tests of endurance of that time, including The Pony Express race in 1979. By the end of this race, every rider had their horse in Easyboots having seen the competitive edge it gave Dr Glass!

Boots like the Easyboot were indeed revolutionary, but I feel it is really in the last decade or so that interest in boot design has moved to a different level, as more manufacturers have taken up the challenge to produce the ultimate in hoof protection. Modern boots are lighter, sleeker and even easier to use than formerly, and there are horses competing successfully to the highest levels, particularly in the discipline of endurance riding, using some of the most modern designs. The performance hoof boot market is still a young and certainly dynamic one, with manufacturers bringing out new models based on new ideas all the time.

Hoof boots differ greatly from all kinds of fixed shoes. The nails or glue used to attach a shoe to the hoof gives no support to the sole, thus producing the effect of peripheral loading, especially as the hoof grows and the outer wall becomes longer. Boots, however, allow the hoof to be trimmed far more regularly, and provide a flat surface as a base that the horse's hoof sits on. Thus, they not only give total protection to the sole but, with the use of specialist pads inside the boots, replicate the support and feedback that the horse would receive when worked barefoot on good going, such as soft turf or any other surface that offers solar support.

The fastenings on hoof boots are usually such that the boot is able to flex or move, or the fastening is able to flex and move with the horse's hoof capsule as it expands and contracts, thus allowing the hoof to work naturally. Horses will usually land heel first almost immediately in a boot, even if they did not do so in a metal shoe, immediately allowing the hoof to work more effectively, increasing circulation and building up the digital cushion more rapidly. This is one of the reasons why they are so valuable in the transitional phase when taking a horse out of shoes, or when rehabilitating a badly trimmed horse.

Some form of solar support should always be used in any hoof boot to help reduce or prevent peripheral loading. Pads will help to provide the ideal surface for every step your horse takes, and will help the hoof to heal and improve while keeping him completely comfortable.

New boots will quickly wear to complement your horse's natural action. The toe will usually develop a quicker breakover and sometimes the heel will wear too. Some people will use a rasp to quicken the breakover on a boot when it is brand new to save waiting for this wear to occur.

Not substitutes for dietary or trimming deficiencies

When moving from shod to barefoot, boots with the correct pads will, in most cases, allow the horse to continue to work to the same level as when shod, whilst exercising and improving the hoof, thus speeding the transition along in the process. One thing that I have to stress, however, is that boots are *not* a substitute for dietary failings or a poor trim. Even with the foundations of a good diet and exercise, a poor trim, such as a traditional pasture trim, will leave the hoof in a weakened and unnatural shape, often with flare combined with overly high or overly low heels, and often a long toe.

There are many hoof boots available, and it may be possible to find a boot to fit the shape of such a hoof, but boots will never work as well as when they are used on an anatomically trimmed, healthy, bare hoof. If your horse has a poor trim, you are far more likely to experience a lost or twisted boot, as a hoof boot, just like any piece of equipment, will only work properly if the boot is the correct size and shape for the hoof. Hooves that are in a poor state, but being worked on, are of course also harder to boot, and you would be wise to get professional help from a specialist to ensure you get the best fit possible. There will have to be compromises with the fit, but you would not be expecting your horse to do too much at first if his feet are in need of a great deal of work, so it is usually possible to get a satisfactory fit for the level of work or for turnout until the hooves have become a more natural shape.

The best boot is the one that fits the size and shape of your horse's hoof best.

Trend towards greater use

I feel that hoof boots are often under-utilised in the UK, even by some hoof care professionals. In parts of Europe such as Germany, and in the USA, boots are used routinely in the transitional phase to barefoot. As mentioned in Chapter 4, Pete Ramey, the widely respected American natural hoof-care practitioner and qualified farrier, became a convert when he decided one day to try booting every horse that came out of shoes for at least a short time. He quickly discovered that booting with pads during at least the first few weeks resulted in a much shorter transitional period, with no discomfort for the horse. He also reported that the owners were happier, as they could continue to do what they wanted to with the horse with no break in work – and, of course, the exercise is no small part of what helps the horses to make the transition so quickly! Ramey now has a policy of supplying boots, often on loan for a few weeks, for each new equine hoof care client he takes on.

I feel that one reason for the resistance to booting we still see some-times in the UK is the memory of the older models that would twist or fall off whilst out on a ride, leaving the rider either having to get on and off to correct the boot, or having to spend a few hours retracing their steps in order to pick up a lost boot! With the wider range of boots on the market today, and a better understanding of a natural hoof shape, a correctly fitting hoof boot will allow your horse to match anything that a shod horse can do. There are now also companies and individuals specialising in hoof boots, and a few will be willing to either come and fit them for you, or give you very accurate advice if you send them your horse's measurements – so long as your measurements *are* accurate, of course! Good hoof care professionals will carry some boots with them for you to try or hire, which is a very handy way to obtain them, as the hoof care professional will be able to ensure that the boots fit properly.

There is a boot to fit almost every hoof, from the smallest to the greatest!

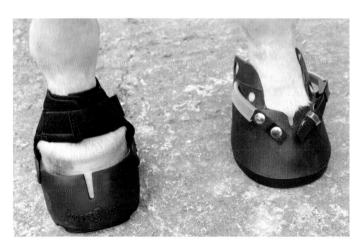

Boots have come a long way in the last 30 years; the Swiss Hoof Boot (right) was one of the first boots made and does require heat fitting, but still sells well today. The boot on the left is the form-fitting Easyboot Glove, used by many endurance riders. Fitting below the hairline, the Glove is known to be one of the best-performing boots at sustained speed – although equally suitable for the happy hacker!

Chapter EIGHT

HOW TO CHOOSE THE RIGHT BOOTS

As SOON AS YOU DECIDE YOU would like to take your horse barefoot, you can begin to look at boots for him. However, all hoof boots will require you to take the measurements of your horse's hooves after a fresh trim so, if the horse has shoes on, you may have to wait until after that first trim to be able to make your purchase. Ideally, your hoof care professional will have boots and pads with them, which will ensure that your horse can go straight into his new boots without a gap, if need be.

Newly de-shod hooves will often have a longer hoof capsule to begin with owing to the lack of stimulus to the sole causing the internal structures to become lower. This can cause an issue with fitting of some hoof boots.

Most horses with reasonable hooves before having their shoes removed will be sound at pasture, which will give you a couple of days to obtain boots if you cannot get them straight away. If you feel your horse is going to struggle without any hoof protection when the shoes come off, it is possible to take measurements of the hoof under the shoe to get a rough idea, but bear in mind that boots ordered through this method are not likely to fit to their optimum, so a different pair may be required for ridden work once the horse's hooves have been trimmed.

The key point to remember when selecting boots is fit. If a boot fits, you will 'fit it and forget it', but if you choose one that is not the best size or shape for your horse's hoof, be prepared for the boot to move, twist or even come off. If you are unsure, ask for help from your hoof care professional, retailer, or the manufacturer. Like saddles, hoof boots are specialist items, but if your horse has a well-shaped hoof, you should find it quite easy to select a boot yourself. If, however, the hooves are not a matching pair, or the hoof has flare or is asymmetrical, it is wise to get some expert help to prevent you going through a few pairs of boots before finding the perfect one!

Every boot is made to fit a slightly different size or shape of hoof, depending on the findings of the manufacturer when they researched their sizing guides for a particular model. This works out nicely for the horse owner as, like people, horses do not necessarily have each hoof the same size and shape. Again, like people, it is not possible to ascertain foot size from height; every person and every equine is an individual! While it is certainly a good idea to look at what is available, you must focus on what will fit your horse best, and not choose based on aesthetics. A beautiful-looking hoof boot that keeps falling off will soon lose its appeal, whereas a design you were less keen on, but which stays in place through mud, water and gives good grip on the road will be worth the cosmetic sacrifice!

The Easyboot Glove is unusual in having a 'fit kit' that allows you to try the various shells to ascertain the correct size. Fit is crucial to success of any hoof boot.

Measuring the hooves for boots

When selecting boots for your horse, the first thing you need to do is measure the hoof. All good hoof boots will require you to take a width and a length measurement to ensure that the boot fits well. I always ask for measurements to be taken in millimetres, as this is the most accurate way to measure for boots and most boots are sized in metric, with only a conversion to inches for their charts, which is less than ideal. Boots that only require one measurement should be looked upon with caution as a hoof that is disproportionately wide or long will encounter problems, but there is no way of knowing this until it is too late and you have purchased the wrong size!

All boots are made to fit a freshly trimmed hoof and have a growth tolerance built into them, so make sure you measure as soon as possible after a fresh trim, and certainly within 10 days. If seeking advice, you should always state the length of time since a fresh trim and whether your horse wears his hooves down between trims so that the booting adviser can take into consideration any growth there may be when selecting the best boot for your horse. As hoof boots are made to fit barefoot horses, their growth tolerance will be on average suitable for 3–6 weeks maximum. Form-fitting performance boots such as the Easyboot Glove will be at the lower end of this scale, whereas more adjustable boots with fastenings will usually allow for more.

The width of the hoof should be taken at the widest point; the length is taken to the *buttress* of the heel, both to the nearest millimetre. Do not include the frog/fleshy part of the heel. It is helpful to hold a straight edge across the back of the bottom edge of the heel buttresses and then measure from the toe, bisecting the frog to the line you have formed. The length can be tricky to measure accurately in some horses, particularly those just out of shoes, since they will have a tendency to long, short or under-run heels, which will give a false length. The heel should emerge out of the heel bulb and be relatively short, only growing a few degrees towards the toe. If your horse has incorrect heels when you measure, you need to measure the length to where the heel would be in a healthy hoof, otherwise you risk the boots being too short.

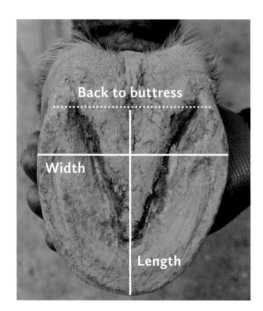

Most horses will measure the same length and width, or slightly longer than wide. If your horse's measurements indicate a hoof wider than it is long, or he has a very long, narrow hoof, it would be wise to get some advice from the company or a professional as to which boots will work, and supplying photos of the hooves (if you are not able to get someone to bring boots to you) will be very helpful to the person advising. Photos of the hooves need to be taken when they are clean inside and out, and the horse should be in a well-lit, clean and flat area such as the yard or stable. Also make sure your horse stays still – there is nothing worse than a fuzzy photo of a dirty

How to measure your horse's hoof for hoof boots. Note that the length measurement is only taken to the buttress of the hoof, not to the back of the heel bulb.

hoof – it won't tell the adviser anything! There are three angles to take; one from straight on of the pair of hooves, then one of the side and sole of each hoof you want to boot. This will allow the adviser to see the shape of the whole hoof to ensure that the boot will fit the higher portions of the hoof as well as the sole (this is particularly important if the horse currently has issues such as flare, which can prevent some boots from working properly even though the measurements may fit the size chart).

Choosing the best hoof boots

Once you have your horse's measurements, you can begin to look for suitable boots. You may have a style in mind; if so, compare your horse's measurements to the chart to see if they are suitable. If the measurements are not within one size, in both width and length, you are best to look to other styles to see if there is something more suitable. Most hoof boots are designed to fit a round or slightly longer than wide hoof, as this is the shape of a lot of horses' hooves when correctly barefoot trimmed.

Thoroughbreds just out of shoes, and some heavier horses, may have a naturally wider than long hoof, so a more specialist boot may be required and the choice will be limited. If all else fails, there are companies that will make boots to measure for individual hooves, but this can be costly so it is best to ensure the hoof is at its optimum size and shape before ordering, as you don't want the horse to change shape in the months following or the boots will have been a waste of money!

With well-trimmed hooves, you will often find the horse will suit more than one style of boot, in which case you can then assess the merits of the various boots and decide which you like the look of. When choosing boots, like most things in life, you do get what you pay for. Be wary of boots that are very cheap; they are often inferior copies that will not stand up to heavy wear and will be difficult to get to fit well, making them far more likely to move or come off, particularly at faster gaits.

There are two categories that boots tend to fall into: boots that fit above the hairline and boots that fit below the hairline. Soft 'gaiter' style fastenings are not included in this description, so boots such as Easyboot Epic or Renegades are regarded as fitting 'below' the hairline. These boots are generally the most suitable for hard, competitive or long-distance use, but are also generally the most sensitive to incorrect sizing and fitting. Boots that are one piece and cover the coronet band such as Old Mac G2 or Easyboot Trail boots are generally easier to size and more tolerant to slight size inaccuracies but, if used without protective gaiters, they may rub some horses when used for distances in excess of 25 miles. However, a lot depends on how well the boot fits and how prone the horse is to rubbing.

Examples of some boots that fit above the hairline (from left to right) Cavallo, Old Mac G2, Easyboot Trail, Swiss Hoof Boot.

Examples of hoof boots that fit below the hairline (from left to right) Marquis Supergrip, Easyboot, Easyboot Glove, Easyboot Epic, Renegade.

Whichever style of boot you consider, there are certain qualities to look for when selecting a suitable hoof boot for your horse. These include:

Weight: A hoof boot should be as light as possible, just the same as running shoes for athletes.

Grip: What is required is a good all-round grip that will not be too aggressive, but will ensure your horse has good traction on roads, grass and mud. Patterns similar to walking boots often offer the best all-round grip on horse boots too – they do not have to be hoof-shaped, as the hoof is on a flat platform inside the boot and a 'whole sole' grip with around 60 per cent tread to space is usually most effective. Metal should not be a part of the sole unless as a fastening.

The way the boot is held on: Simple, easy-to-use fastenings are best. Some boots, such as the Easyboot Glove, have even done away with the need for fastening all together. Avoid boots that put pressure in one place, and look for something that will enable you to get a really close fit.

Materials: A good hoof boot will be made of modern materials, with a sole made from a plastic/rubber composite to give good grip and durability. The upper should be soft above the hairline, but may be made of a flexible plastic/rubber similar to the sole around the hoof capsule. There should be no metal in contact with the horse's hoof.

Manufacturer's reputation: A good way to see how well a hoof boot performs is to see how many horses are using them. If a boot is being used by top riders, or getting good reports on equine forums from other users, then it is a pretty safe bet that it is a well-designed boot that, when correctly fitted, will do a good job.

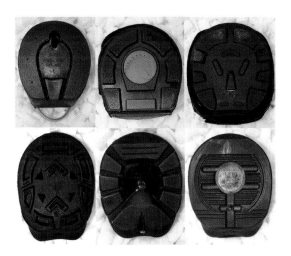

When considering a boot, choose a sole appropriate to the ground conditions you will be riding on. A good general-purpose sole with a tread that offers grip without being too aggressive is usually a sound choice for road and tracks.

Some boots open right out to facilitate putting them on, and can be fastened with the foot flat on the ground. This can be a benefit for young horses that lack patience or older horses that find it uncomfortable to stand on three legs for any length of time.

Popular hoof boots

There are many types of boot on the market, but very few specialist manufacturers. Most companies are small manufacturers producing their own style of boot based on their own research. At the time of writing there are no widely used UK-designed hoof boots; American and European manufacturers supply the largest volume of boots, using distributors in the UK to offer the stock and back-up to UK customers. The best-known and largest global producer is Easycare Inc., a company based in the US with distributors around the world; their products can be purchased through trimmers, tack shops and online (with some dealers offering hire of the boots). Easycare produces a wide range of boots catering for different hoof shapes and sizes in different styles to accommodate most hoof shapes. Garrett Ford, their CEO, and other members of their team, are often to be seen showing what their horses can do in their boots at major competitions, and they fund research projects into the benefits of keeping horses barefoot.

Another highly successful boot from the USA is the Renegade, designed by Kurt Lander. This boot is not so easily available, as Mr Lander is less keen to sell his boots through retailers, preferring to offer the advice to fit them either himself or through specialists such as trimmers. Marquis boots, from Germany, are available through an independent supplier in the UK for hire and purchase, and comprehensive advice on their particular boots is available for fitting and use. Swiss Hoof Boots, one of the original boots, are available direct from the manufacturer in Switzerland, but are slightly more specialised as they require heat fitting to obtain a really good fit. Hoofwings, another US company with a UK representative, produce a boot that can be made to measure and this is a good boot for those with difficult hooves to fit.

This is by no means an exhaustive list, and new boots are coming on to the market all the time. The internet is a very good place to find the different makes and most manufacturers will post worldwide if you particularly like a certain boot.

How to tell if a boot fits

Obviously, careful measurement of the foot, as described earlier, is the most important criterion for achieving a good fit but, as with human footwear and clothing, nothing is certain until the 'trying on' stage.

Once you have selected a boot for your horse, fit the boot as per the manufacturer's instructions, and see how it fits. Does it go on easily? Does the hoof fill the inside of the boot nicely without bulging or causing any 'gapping' in the fastenings? Check that the fastenings are not too tight; think of your horse's footwear as you would your own – ensure that any potential pressure points, such as airbags or clasps, are no tighter than anywhere else. When the boot is on the hoof, you shouldn't be able to twist it from side to side by any more than around 5 degrees (unless stated differently by the individual manufacturer), as this could indicate that the boot could be too big, or the wrong shape for the horse's hoof.

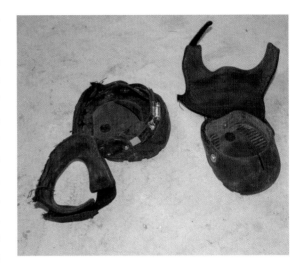

Correct fit is vital to the success of any hoof boot. If the boot is too long, the breakover will be increased, predisposing the horse to overreaching and treading on the front boots and causing damage or loss of a boot.

It is important to make sure that boots are not over-tightened (although most boots are difficult to over-tighten by hand). Where boots rely on airbags to stay on, care must be taken not to over-inflate the air bags, or bruising or hair loss can occur.

The 'wiggle test' is a useful way to test the fit of boots. With most boots that fit above the hairline there should be no more than 5 degrees of movement when trying to twist them. Boots that fit below the hairline should ideally have no movement.

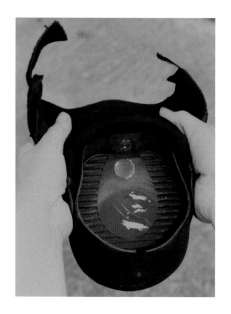

If it is difficult to get the boot on, it may be too small, so try the next size up. This also applies if you find the fastenings are only just doing up, or are at the end of their tolerance. Sometimes, for example, a horse will have a small hoof in relation to the pastern, in which case he is usually better with the smaller size – but comparing with the larger size is usually enough to make the decision an easy one. If you are not sure, ask the retailer or manufacturer for guidance, as usually once you have used the boots, you will not be able to return them for an exchange or refund (unless you have hired them or they come with some kind of money-back guarantee).

When using a boot with a gaiter attached, ensuring that the gaiter is opened right out will make application much easier.

The importance of pads

One area often overlooked is the use of pads in hoof boots. Good hoof boot manufacturers will produce pads that you can fit into their boots and, to my mind, the pads should be considered as a necessity and not an option for most horses. Hoof boots all have a flat surface inside, which will promote peripheral loading – which is what we are working so hard to avoid with our barefoot horses! When moving on any soft, sandy or even dusty/gritty surface, the hoof will fill with the ground material to support the solar dome and help prevent the potentially detrimental peripheral loading, and pads mimic this support and stimulation by filling the underside of the hoof.

Pads are also the key to improving a poor hoof, helping to increase circulation, or conditioning a horse to work on stony surfaces.

Dr Robert Bowker's Dopplar Ultrasound studies have shown that the greater the peripheral loading, the worse the blood flow throughout the hoof capsule. One of the best surfaces to help improve blood flow through a horse's hoof is pea gravel, and Dr Bowker performed an independent test of different materials including Easycare's medium density 12mm foam pads.[14] By using the right pads for your horse, you can help to replicate this support, making sure every step your horse takes is on an 'ideal' surface, whilst helping to reduce concussion and increase circulation. Pads need to be thick enough to fill the underside of the hoof, so anything les than 6mm is usually not going to be of much use. I like to use 12mm pads as I find they offer the optimum support for most horses with at least some concavity. Density is also a consideration; a soft pad is useful for laminitic horses or very small equines, and hard pads are more suited to very large horses.

There are also more specialist pads such as frog support pads and 'sole mates' – a 1in (25mm) thick pad used by some hoof care professionals – which can help to stimulate and improve the frog and sole and provide support in the case of disease or injury, but these should only ever be used with guidance from a professional.

It can equally be argued that a barefoot horse is actually better off wearing correctly padded hoof boots for all work on flat surfaces (such as the road) since such work will predispose the horse to the undesirable loss of blood flow owing to peripheral loading. Horses that live on flat surfaces, such as a group of youngsters kept in a barn with a yard for the winter, will, however, begin to adapt to this new surface by 'losing' concavity as the sole adapts to the lack of direct stimulation. This is another good example of how the hoof will naturally adapt to a set of circumstances when given the chance.

A comfort pad is cut to fit and sits in the bottom of the boot. A thinner pad is used in close-fitting boots such as those that fit below the hairline; the thicker pads to condition the hoof are usually only suitable for boots that fit over the hair-line as the pad can cause movement in the boot, which can affect the fit of very tight-fitting boots.

Reference
14. www.thehorseshoof.com/Art_Pad.html (No link available to the original study.)

Chapter NINE

LONG-TERM HOOF BOOT CARE AND USE

HOOF BOOTS ARE LIKE ANY other piece of tack or equipment you use on your horse, and should be cared for to get the best from them. After each use, the boots should have the worst of the mud removed from them (a good hose-down or dunk in a bucket of water will usually do this very quickly!), and the inside should be checked for small stones/gravel and any lumps of mud or deposits that could cause rubbing.

The boots should be routinely inspected for signs of wear, any screws or fittings checked for tightness, and cables or buckles checked for signs of stress or fraying. Just like all tack, damaged boots should not be used until the problem has been rectified, or they have been checked by a knowledgeable individual for safety. It is also worth measuring your horse's hooves every couple of months, especially during the transitional period, to monitor your horse's foot shape/size (as they can change), just to make sure the boots are still the best boots for your horse!

Online auction sites are a very easy way to buy and sell used boots, and often good prices can be made if you do need to sell your boots on, and replace them with a different pair.

If you are using one pair of boots on more than one horse, it is wise to use a disinfectant spray in between horses, to prevent the spread of infection. Something akin to the spray used to disinfect shoes at a bowling alley can, for example, be used, or there are specialist hoof disinfectant sprays on the market. At least once a week pads should be removed and the boot and pad should be sprayed liberally, before returning the pad to the boot. Obviously it is important only to use a hoof boot on a horse if it fits the hoof in question

Common booting problems and questions

With all makes and models of boots, you could encounter a problem, but this is usually to do with either the boot not being the best fit, or the horse's hoof not being in the best condition at the time. Sometimes, especially when going barefoot after a hoof problem or poor shoeing, you will have to compromise with the fit, which will make it more likely to fail. There is often a way to help fit on most occasions with most makes of boot; the manufacturer or retailer will usually be very helpful and able to advise on your horse's individual needs. (Again, make sure you supply *current* measurements if seeking help, and also the type of boot you are using and any gait or conformation abnormalities your horse may have, such as dishing or being pigeon-toed.)

Twisting

Twisting can be a simple indication that the boot is either the wrong shape or too big; if you are able to twist the boot yourself more than around 5 degrees when the horse's foot is up, one or other of these is the likely cause, and a smaller size or alternative model should be tried. It goes without saying that the better the boot fits, the less likely it is to twist, but if the horse has a natural twist in his gait (common in hind feet, or horses that dish), the correct fit is even more important, as the horse will be exerting unnatural pressure on the boot which may cause it to move.

If the boot fits well but still twists, you need to try to get the boot, and especially the width, as tight (without causing restriction) as possible. Some manufacturers, such as Old Macs, produce specially designed inserts that fix in the side of the boots to allow a tighter fit on the width at the top of the hoof.

Brushing can also twist a boot; if your horse's legs move close together, using thick brushing boots or fetlock boots behind, such as sheepskin-lined versions or even a sausage boot, will usually keep the coronet

bands far enough apart to prevent the horse from catching the boot and knocking them off centre.

Boots that are too wide or too big may cause your horse to brush and damage the boot. Brushing can also cause a boot to twist. The wrinkling at the top of this boot and the damage to the strap would suggest that this horse would benefit from possibly a smaller, certainly less deep, boot with a slimmer profile. However well made a boot, it may be damaged if it doesn't fit a particular horse properly.

Rubbing

Rubbing will often occur if the boot is too small, the wrong model, or fastened too loosely – check your measurements again and try a different model or the next size up to see if that fits better. Make sure the foot is

Placing the sole of the hoof against the sole of the boot, can help you to see if the hoof will sit flat on the sole of the boot inside. Just remember to allow a few millimetres for the wall of the boot; the hoof should sit just within the sole all the way around.

really on the sole of the boot, and not crushing the heel. One way to check the length of the hoof inside the boot is to put the sole of the foot flat on the outside of the sole of the boot; this will show you exactly where the hoof is sitting inside the boot. If there is any overhang it is pretty safe to say that the hoof is not able to sit flat comfortably inside the boot, which can cause rubbing, as the upper will be under more strain.

Rubbing is usually more common in horses with under-run heels, where the measurements for length have not taken the under-run heels into consideration, thus making the bulb of the heel 'larger' than anticipated, and the boot too short.

Boots that fit above the coronet band have the potential to rub, as they are making contact with softer parts of the horse's hoof and leg; some boots have special wraps or gaiters that act as 'socks' to help protect sensitive skin. Just like humans with new shoes, your horse will need a period of adjustment to wearing boots, not only to break the boots in, but also to allow the horse's body to become accustomed to them, like our own feet do. For boots that do not have their own 'socks', you can experiment with a fine woollen sock, elasticated support bandage (tube-grip) or cohesive wrap, to find out what works best for your horse. However, you should only try these solutions when you are sure the size and fit are correct, and the only issue is that your horse is particularly sensitive, the boots are new/your horse is not used to wearing them, or you are doing a lot of miles in them.

Horse still sensitive with boots

If, after carrying out all the checks on fit, your horse is still reluctant to walk with boots on, and you have not already done so, you should consult your vet to rule out the possibility of laminitis or any other problem. All boots should ideally be used with solar support comfort pads such as 12mm medium or soft foam pads although 1in (25mm) thick 'sole mate' type pads work best for very sore horses.

Lost or broken boots

All good hoof boots are made to withstand the weight of a horse and the pressures generated over miles of rugged terrain, but just as a horse can rip off a metal shoe, it is possible to lose a boot. If you lose a boot within the first week, or more than once in the first month, it is most likely the wrong style/shape/size for your horse's hooves, and you should check the fit with the manufacturer or knowledgeable retailer first, to see if another size or style may be more appropriate.

Boots that fit above the hairline are usually easier to fit and more tolerant of different hoof shapes, but can be more likely to cause rubs on some horses. A neoprene gaiter that can be used inside the boot acts like a sock in a shoe to help alleviate any rubbing. Gaiters are also useful to make a slightly roomy hoof boot fit more closely, and can help to prevent twisting.

A common cause for lost boots is for the boot to be too long (foot length measurement). This occurs particularly with hooves wider than they are long, that are booted in front boots designed for round or 'longer than wide' hooves. This fit increases the breakover, allowing the hind foot to come through and tread on the back of the boot, which can rip it off. If a shorter front boot is not possible (for example, the horse has overly long toes that cannot be shortened at present), booting the hind feet can help to even out the breakover a little. Overreach boots can also help.

Most hoof boots are not designed for turnout, only riding, as they are more likely to be damaged in the field. A horse at liberty is more likely to leap about and roll, and is more likely to tread on himself or catch a boot than a horse under saddle. Hence, the chance of damage is greater in the field. If you need to turn out in boots, choosing a boot that is designed specifically for turnout, or that fits securely above the hairline, usually works best.

Hoof boots with a very large gap around the pastern should be avoided as they will make the boot more prone to being lost in mud, sand and water as well as allowing small stones and grit to enter the boot, which could make the horse sore.

Specialist boots for poulticing, medicating and soaking can be invaluable and, in some cases, can be used for light turnout, but are not designed for ridden work. Not only must the boot fit, but make sure it is the right one for the job!

Watch out for uneven wear – this can sometimes be a sign of an imbalance in the trim. Whatever the cause, it is usually best to correct any imbalances that appear in the boots, or replace them to prevent the boot exacerbating the problem.

Boots wear unevenly or wear out quickly

Most boots will last far longer than metal shoes, but as all horses wear shoes differently, it is the same with boots. If the wear is uneven, you need to make sure you know the reason for this, so talk to your hoof care professional, and discuss whether this is normal and correct for your horse, or if it could be a symptom of something that needs addressing. Heavy wear on the toe, or toe-dragging, can be a symptom of an overly long toe, or even arthritis further up the leg, so it is best to get the horse checked to rule out any physical problems.

The toes of boots can often be reinforced by gluing a piece of rawhide or similar material to the front, which can then be replaced when it has worn away. It should be noted that the sole of an uneven boot should be rebalanced with a rasp (or, if possible alternate the boots on the hooves) just as you would a horse's hoof, to ensure no imbalances creep in to the boot and therefore the hoof or leg.

Can boots be used over metal shoes?

Some hoof boots can be used over metal shoes, but you should check whether this will invalidate any manufacturer's warranty first. It must be noted that booting over metal shoes (even with pads) is of little benefit to the horse, other than to enhance grip and protect the sole from penetration, and will not absorb significant amounts of shock; removing the metal shoes first is the only way to do this!

Won't my horse come to rely on boots, so I will always have to use them?

No – actually the opposite is the case! Hoof boots with pads will help to improve your horse's hooves, whilst keeping him comfortable and allowing you to exercise him; you can begin to take the horse out for short rides without boots once his feet are at a suitable stage, and this can gradually be built up to the stage where you do not need the boots. This will, of course, depend on the terrain you are riding on, and how much work you are managing to do with your horse, as well as how good the diet is and the condition of the hooves; some horses may always need boots to work confidently on some surfaces, but most are able to come out of boots permanently on a really good barefoot regime. Just keep in mind that, if you do go somewhere different and are not aware of the terrain, it is best to boot up just in case it is rougher than your horse is used to. So don't ditch your boots for a while, even if you think you won't need them again, just in case!

Are there hoof boots to fit every horse?

There are hoof boots on the market to fit all sizes from very small ponies up to very large heavy horses, and there are a few companies that will make to measure; so in theory, there shouldn't be a horse that you couldn't find boots for, if you wanted to! The problem is that made-to-measure boots can be expensive, and they are all designed to fit a naturally trimmed hoof, so it can be trickier to boot hooves with pathologies or abnormalities. Some boots, such as the Swiss Hoof Boots and the Easyboot Glove, can be heat-fitted around the most difficult hoof shapes as a temporary measure, and a good hoof care professional will be able to help you with this.

Chapter TEN

CASE STUDIES

THIS FINAL CHAPTER CONSISTS OF some question and answer sess-
ions with owners who have decided to take their horses down the
barefoot route. I hope it provides some insights into why owners may
make this choice, and what can be achieved.

HORSE · Bapsford (17-year-old TB gelding)

How long has your horse been barefoot?

Since September 2010.

Why did you go barefoot?

I have owned Bapsford since 2001 and in that time he has been fairly
accident-prone; on two occasions he damaged the medial suspensory
ligament of his left hind leg, and required lengthy periods of box rest.
Each time, it has then triggered lameness problems relating to his hips
and sacro-iliac joint. In March 2010, he spooked on the road and skidded,
nearly falling over, and went lame on his right fore. He had sprained his
coffin joint. Again, more box rest! And again he then had lameness issues
with his hind limbs and back. This time osteopathy alone did not seem to
be helping. I had started to read my friend's natural horsemanship maga-
zines at this time and read an article about going barefoot; it seemed like

Bapsford is one of many Thoroughbreds that have successfully gone barefoot; breed is no obstacle if you are determined to give your horse healthy hooves!

this could be something that could help. At first I thought it would not be possible as surely his feet would not be able to cope with the amount of roadwork I needed to do (we have very little off-road hacking). But the more I started to research, the more I realised that I had nothing to lose by trying it; he was not sound enough to ride properly with shoes on anyway.

What are the main advantages you have found?

I have a sound horse again! His typical Thoroughbred flat feet have transformed into nice neat upright feet with improved grip – so no more slipping on the roads and I could ride in the snow. I am no longer paranoid about the hard ground, knowing that he has proper, natural shock-absorbers protecting his legs now. Obviously it is cheaper than being shod, which is a bonus, but this would never be the reason I made the decision. Oh, and no more lost shoes! He can also live as part of a herd without the worry of the horses injuring each other [through kicking]. Overall, I have a much happier horse.

Thoroughbreds are renowned for having flat, weak feet but Bapsford proves that given the right diet, management and trim it will allow 'even Thoroughbreds' to grow a thick sole with lovely open heels and a nice full frog.

Do you ever use barefoot boots – if so, which ones?

I did buy the Old Mac G2s for his front feet to help during the transition, but I only used them a handful of times. I forgot to put them on one day and went off on quite a long ride – I only realised when we got back, as he went so well! So they have become redundant.

Have you had resistance from farriers/vets?

I am a vet in small animal practice and am shocked about how little I knew about the proper function of the hoof and how horseshoes prevent this. When I told my farrier (of 20 years) what I was planning, he said, 'Well of course it is better for their feet if you don't shoe them, but I'd be surprised if you can do that much roadwork'; however he is used to me trying to prove him wrong and has remained supportive! When I told my equine vet why he'd not seen us for lameness issues for some time, he was pleased and said he knew of more people that were not shoeing now.

Who trims your horse – is it a farrier, yourself or a trimmer (if so, which association)?

My farrier removed my horse's shoes and did an initial pasture trim to balance his feet, however I was keen to try looking after his feet myself, so since then I have been following Jamie Jackson and Pete Ramey's books and rasping the feet myself. It is much easier to do a 'tidy up' rasp every three or four weeks and when we are doing plenty of roadwork there isn't too much for me to do. I've subsequently removed my driving Shetland's shoes and trim him myself also. I would like to do one of the trimming courses in the future.

What do you and your horse do together?

Mostly hacking, and since last summer we have started doing horse agility. Last month we did our first Trec training session, where he excelled himself, and we are about to compete in our first Trec competition. Since going barefoot, I have also gone bitless, and have found the confidence to start a bit of jumping again.

Anything else of relevance you want to add?

Having seen how well Bapsford is going now, two of my friends have decided to try their horses barefoot, in particular after seeing how well he can come down steep tarmac roads without slipping all over the place! People have also noticed how much better the horse uses his back legs. I feel we have to lead by example and educate people that horses do not need to be shod to be ridden or driven.

HORSE · Joe (12-year-old Welsh Section D)

How long has your horse been barefoot?

Since 2009.

Why did you go barefoot?

Joe was diagnosed with coffin joint arthritis, navicular syndrome and ring-bone in both forelegs in February 2008. I spent the next six months trying different treatments, both medicinal and remedial.

One of the main concerns during this time was the fact that Joe was not responding to the prescribed remedial shoeing. He was tried with heart-bar shoes and silicone pads, but unfortunately this proved to be a problem owing to Joe being lame for up to 5 days following every shoeing, then subsequently losing the shoes within 10–14 days – this created a vicious circle that stopped any recovery.

During this time, Joe was given one sachet of a non-steroidal anti-inflammatory drug (NSAID) a day, and then two daily for the 7 days around shoeing. It was eventually decided that this treatment was not sustainable, and that Joe should be retired to live in the field; once retired to the field he still required half a sachet a day to keep him comfortable.

On his first viewing of Joe, trimmer Steven Leigh of Nature's Way Natural Hoof Care, said it was apparent that the horse was not only bilaterally lame in walk, but also could not stand comfortably squarely anywhere. It was obvious that, to become comfortable, he also had to move correctly again with a heel-first landing. The current diet was checked and found to look ideal, so was not changed at this time.

'It is important to remember that a horse needs to be comfortable to move correctly; a sore horse won't want to move much, so this is a key aspect to any rehabilitation', says Stephen. 'Any trimming should be as minimal as possible, and done so over time in line with what the horse needs and develops – not simply at set intervals, whether the horse needs it or not – I strongly believe that any trim is about helping the horse create the hoof structure and balance it needs itself, not forcing one upon it again.'

What are the main advantages you have found?

From the very first trim, Joe moved better and no longer required any NSAIDs, which was a fantastic step forward. Eighteen months on, and Joe

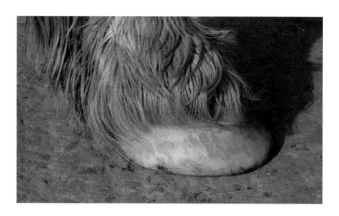

ABOVE *Before Steve had started to trim, this horse had many problems including navicular and ringbone.*

ABOVE RIGHT *Nine months on (and with feathers grown back!) a dramatic difference in the hooves, which is just one small part of the enormous difference a knowledgeable hoof care professional can make to a horse.*

is now moving much more correctly, landing heel first, and lightly hacking out completely barefoot.

Do you ever use barefoot boots?

Stephen advised that while hoof boots and pads are an excellent aid, during the first 9 months it was best to allow Joe to live out and progress at his own pace; he was not footsore, so they were not required at this stage.

During this period, the horse's hooves improved noticeably, including redeveloping some concavity to the soles. After this time, it was decided to walk Joe out in hoof boots and pads for short periods; after 3 weeks of regular walks, Joe was ridden out for the first time in hoof boots, and over the next few months, this was built up.

Is there anything you'd like to add?

According to Steven Leigh, a barefoot regime helps simply because the hoof is designed to work in an optimum way; and ensuring that it develops and functions correctly allows the horse to move and carry itself properly again. 'The lameness-causing stresses are then relieved from the joints and structures that are not designed to take them in the way they were previously being applied – it sounds complicated, but it's actually a simple concept once you take time to think about it', Stephen explains. 'A lame horse will not move correctly and a horse that is not moving correctly will most likely be or become lame; it's a vicious circle. Barefoot boots, as well as supplements and nutritional products that help balance the equine gut, are all available to help the horse help itself.

HORSE · Mac (17-year-old Cob)

How long has your horse been barefoot?

Since 2009.

Why did you go barefoot?

Having ridden Mac for several years, I couldn't resist buying him two years ago, at the age of 15, despite his retirement being on health grounds, and knowing he was arthritic and apparently short-winded. Definitely a 'heart over head' moment! The latter was quickly dismissed, quite correctly, by my vet as lack of fitness, and the arthritis treated with a very expensive but effective supplement.

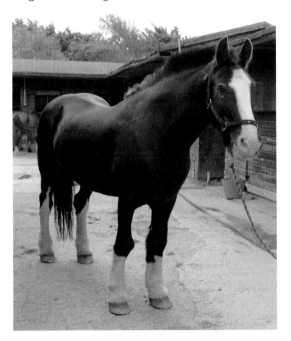

It was on a visit to Adam Goodfellow and Nicole Golding's yard in Gloucestershire to work on some of Mac's other little training issues that I hadn't known about – such as Olympic-standard barging, bucking, napping, extreme fear of being alone – that I decided to go barefoot. This was to help his health in general, and his arthritis in particular, as pain was definitely causing some of his problems. All their horses are barefoot and we had talked previously about the benefits for the horse.

Arthritis and thrush are just two of so many conditions that going barefoot can help. Mac has found new life since his shoes came off!

What are the main advantages you have found?

Mac's been barefoot now for over 18 months, and the benefits are huge! The arthritis, although incurable, is much improved and he no longer needs the expensive supplement, although he does have a herbal cocktail of meadowsweet, comfrey and rosehips. Thrush has become a thing of the past.

He walks, trots and canters over anything but mud. Riding him downhill used to be horrible, like he was walking in stilettos, but now he'll happily trot downhill. His whole movement has become more free, and he's much more willing to go forward – I have to stop him cantering on the road! And he doesn't slip on tarmac, snow or ice! He's actually stopped tripping like he used to, and seems to know that he has a leg and a foot at each corner now. Better still, he can tell when his foot is standing on mine and will move it unasked!

Do you ever use barefoot boots – if so, which ones?

As getting Mac to hold his feet up long enough to put hoof boots on was going to be painful for him, I didn't bother with them, although my new horse has Cavallo Sports boots.

Have you had resistance from farriers/vets?

My decision was met with a certain amount of scepticism, but I actually encountered very little real resistance or negativity; except from a surfer! I was taking Mac for a walk, just for fun, last winter, when the surfer told me rather acidly that I'd forgotten something crucial – the horse's shoes! I assume he was a surfing farrier!

Who trims your horse – is it a farrier, yourself or a trimmer (if so, which association)?

I was put in touch with my trimmer, Ian Whatley, a member of the IAEP, who explained the process of converting [from shod to bare], calmed my fears and gave me the confidence to go ahead. Ian told me that Mac would let me know when he was ready to be ridden, by trotting happily along the roads and tracks, but that Ian would be back to check him before then!

Expecting 3 to 6 months of 'in-hand work' on the roads, I was amazed to find Mac doing a spanking trot along the roads just 6 weeks after his shoes were removed (an awful lot of time was spent walking for miles round the village, improving our fitness), and I was out on short hacks within 2 months.

Ian's been looking after Mac ever since, and I'm always amazed at the patience and gentleness he shows to my stubborn old boy, always acknowledging that lifting feet might hurt and finding the most comfortable position for Mac.

What do you and your horse do together?

Since he's still reluctant to go out hacking alone, rather than try to force Mac to do something he was so very obviously unhappy with, and as he's definitely not ready to retire just yet, I decided to try horse agility. We go to The Mendip Stud for it, and he loves every minute. We have great fun together and we're both learning new skills. He still hacks out with me but his main role is Very Important Partner in agility, and he's a very, very happy horse.

HORSE · Shanti (13-year-old ID x Anglo-Arab)

How long has your horse been barefoot?

Three-and-a-quarter years, since 2008.

Why did you go barefoot?

Mainly because I was worried about concussion from being shod.

What are the main advantages you have found?

I have much more autonomy now over Shanti's hoofcare. When you go barefoot it is a massive learning curve of self-education about hooves, diet and keeping. So I have learnt a great deal about many other areas than I expected to. Other advantages would include feeling much more secure riding on roads than on a shod horse! I find he seems less stiff in his hind legs than he used to. His frogs have improved immeasurably. Shanti's hooves were quite contracted and have now widened and de-contracted at the heels. Also he does not seem to have so many scars and cracks in his hooves and lower legs. After his last endurance ride when shod, he had caught himself with his shoes on the coronet band, and also had several scratches on his lower legs; these do not seem to happen anymore.

Do you ever use barefoot boots – if so, which ones?

I have booted with Easyboot Gloves. Mainly on the front, occasionally on the hind feet, but that was during transition.

Have you had resistance from farriers/vets?

Sadly, yes, I have had some rude comments at endurance rides from farriers. The vets at home seem to assume that I do not ride my horses at all, since I went barefoot.

Who trims your horse – is it a farrier, yourself or a trimmer (if so, which association)?

I use a trimmer from the AANHCP; I also do some maintenance myself in between trims, if necessary.

What do you and your horse do together?

We do endurance, with over 200 competitive miles under our belt since going barefoot after the initial transition period. At the moment we are concentrating on trying to follow some of the principles of classical dressage, in between riding out on Dartmoor.

Anything else of relevance you want to add?

If you are in transition, stick with it and don't forget that diet and management are important parts of the equation.

Vicki and Shanti regularly take part in endurance rides, being active members of EGB, and Vicki is among a growing number of competitive riders who are finding that barefoot is not only better for their horses but can give them the competitive edge.

HORSE · Zahara (Spanish)

How long has your horse been barefoot?

Eight years, since 2003.

Why did you go barefoot?

Zahara had a tendon injury in May 2003 and was turned out for 5 months to heal. That was a good opportunity to take the shoes off and let her hooves recover and adjust.

What are the main advantages you have found?

Apart from saving the costs for new shoes, it makes me feel better because I know that I am not obstructing her hoof mechanism and she is as natural as she can be. Being barefoot makes Zahara more surefooted on any ground. Gone is the fear of sliding on short grass when we had a performance or sliding on the road – or having to calculate when to put in the rubber inserts for the shoes that keep the snow from forming 'stiletto heels'.

Do you ever use barefoot boots – if so, which ones?

In the first half year, I used boots for longer hacks. The tracks around where we used to live are mainly different sizes of gravel with a grass centre strip, and if you are not careful, it can wear the hooves down quite a bit. I used Marquis hoof boots. This is a German brand with an air cushion at the bulb of the hoof that you have to pump up for optimal fit. The disadvantages are that they are quite heavy and you have to take your small pump with you when you ride, in case you lose a boot. I lost one once or twice in full gallop but luckily found it again. After a while it was easier to watch where you ride, than to bother with the boots, and Zahara's feet had become hard enough not to need the boots.

All the exercise Zahara gets means she has tough, strong hooves and no longer needs boots at all.

Have you had resistance from farriers/vets?

I was very lucky to have a very good vet. He always gave me the choice between the different treatments available and their prices instead of going straight for the most expensive one. He also works with homeopathy and acupuncture. I don't remember if he said anything in particular, but what he would have said was, 'You want to take the shoes off? Now is the best time to do it then.'

The farrier I used for shoeing was one of the 'old school' who also shod my yard owner's carriage horses. There were several farriers who came to our yard and I chose one who did a lot of barefoot horses to take the shoes off and do the trimming.

Who trims your horse – is it a farrier, yourself or a trimmer (if so, which association)?

At first, I used a farrier who did both trimming and shoeing. Then I took a course on hoof trimming and started to trim Zahara's hooves myself. I let a trimmer check her hooves twice a year, but usually get the answer, 'There's nothing I need to do, her feet are fine.'

What do you and your horse do together?

We do dressage, side-saddle, showjumping, cross-country jumping, circus tricks, long rein, agility, skill at arms and medieval re-enactment battles.

In everything I do with Zahara, or teach her, I do my best to be gentle and friendly, yet persistent. I prefer to take longer to get a result that is performed with trust and confidence and the necessary physical development than with fear and under tension. And I believe you have to expose your horse to as many different influences as possible to strengthen the horse's nerves and confidence and the horse/rider bond. After all, wouldn't it be boring if we always did the same things?

Zahara shows it is not just dressage and jumping that barefoot horses are good at! Being barefoot gives Zahara more confidence, and no need to worry about slipping on short, wet grass.

INDEX